AF619932

The True Story Of A Man Who Once Struggled With Porn

By Jeffrey Wooden

© 2012, 2014 Son Set Free Ministries

IN
Copyright © 2012, 2014
Son Set Free Ministries

ALL RIGHTS RESERVED

No portion of this publication may be reproduced, stored in any electronic system, or transmitted in any form or by any means, electronic, mechanical, photocopy, recording, or otherwise, without written permission from the author. Please direct inquiry to woodenjeffrey@gmail.com. Brief quotations may be used in literary reviews.

All Scripture quotations are taken from the King James Version of the Bible.

FOR SPEAKING ENGAGEMENTS
OR INQUIRES OF OTHER PRODUCTS
PLEASE CONTACT:

Jeffrey Wooden
woodenjeffrey@gmail.com
417-350-9054

This book is dedicated to all the people who have struggled with addictions in their lives. There is hope.

In Appreciation

…to Majetta Morris who committed many tireless hours to the editing of this book. I deeply appreciate her effort and suggestions. If you need an editor, you may contact her at majettamorris@yahoo.com.

…to Mica Colston for reading and giving his input on the overall "sound" of this book.

…to my wife, Erin, who stuck it out with me during the most challenging times in my life. My love for her is deep.

I could not have done this without all of your help.

…to My Lord and Savior Jesus Christ who provided the means for my deliverance and loved me enough to offer it to me freely.

TABLE OF CONTENTS

DEFINITIONS

Addiction –

An addiction is anything that you are devoted to and places you in a state of bondage.

When I was addicted, this is how I felt –

I tried unsuccessfully to stop. I was constantly pulled into the sin, the bad habit, the ungodly pleasure and seemingly unable to stop. I felt I had no choice but to give in to my addiction. My mind dwelt constantly on the sin and I found pleasure in pursuing it even though I knew it was wrong and hurt others. I wanted to stop but I couldn't. I unsuccessfully tried many methods to at least slow it down. What began as a simple act of disobedience had dug its claws into me and pulled me down to depths of despair and hopelessness. I felt abandoned by God, unable to control myself, and helpless to resist. I knew I must quit but I could not. My will power was useless.

What it means to be free from addiction –

To be free is to no longer be in bondage. To be free is to have the liberty not to sin. Freedom from my addiction means I am not dwelling on or desiring the sin. I no longer think the way I used to think. I live a life of peace, joy, and self-control without self-effort.

My addiction no longer controls me and is as if it never was. Freedom does not mean that temptation will not arise occasionally; however, the temptation has no pull and is dead to me. Living the overcoming life becomes second nature much like getting up in the morning is a natural result of a good night's rest. With the innocence of a two-year old child who has never experienced the bondage, I'm having fun enjoying life.

INTRODUCTION

I had been fighting this war as long as I could remember. The artillery attacking from a safe distance had made a demoralizing impact on my stronghold. Devastation was everywhere, tunnels were caved in and I was all alone in the fortress I had built. I had been fighting for years with no assistance, no encouragement, and no reinforcements. This was just another day in the life of a lonely and weary soldier.

I couldn't let my commander down by giving up the fort and surrendering myself to the enemy. But I was tired; *exhausted* would probably be a better word to describe it. I wanted rest and quiet, peace and comfort, but they were alien to me–only dreams.

I had managed to reach a place where I had a bird's-eye view of the valley below. It was dark and hard to see anything. But I could hear whispering near me. I couldn't make out the words, but it seemed they were getting closer to my position. Then movement in the darkness–something mysterious, something camouflaged. I pulled the pin of a hand grenade and threw it toward what I thought was my adversary. The explosion was mighty permitting me to see shadows for only an instant, but I didn't know if it had the necessary effect. Then in a rage, I spewed gunfire all over the valley, hoping to destroy the shadows. But they persistently fired back at me with renewed vigor and defiance. "Attack! Attack!" The voices of hundreds in unison pushed toward me–the sound of a mighty force that would create fear in anyone. Automatically my arms covered my head in protection as rocks from above loosened by enemy fire began pelting me. Forced to retreat, I moved to safety. Covered in debris, I most certainly gave my position away as I coughed the dust from my lungs.

I retreated deeper into the tunnel, seeking to reinforce my position. I built blockades and created detours, trying to deceive the enemy into thinking the catacombs inside were endless and therefore to give up the search. I set traps and dead-ends. Portions of the fortress were still untouched by the enemy where I could secure my position. I knew they were coming. It was only a matter of time. The enemy surrounded me on all sides, and I needed a place to rest.

Moving deeper into the depths of the earth, I arrived at a place untouched by the enemy. Finally, I had the opportunity to pause to consider my next step and to strategize my next move. Suddenly there was an explosion in the distance–the enemy had set off one of the trip-wires. You could hear the avalanche of rock rumbling onto the enemy in the distance. No one could survive it. A small victory achieved and for me–some temporary relief, at least for now.

CHAPTER 1

Influence

Train up a child in the way he should go: and when he is old, he will not depart from it.
Proverbs 22:6

The impact of the many hours of time and effort a family has on the life of a person can appear to be a waste with no obviously manifested positive results. However, much of what we believe, become, and do in life is the direct result of our rearing. I, the oldest of three children, am blessed because godly parents raised me in a Christian home. Some have not had this benefit, making it more challenging for them to live for God in a negative environment. However, that can't be used as an excuse before God and as a reason for failures. God places us in our environment for a reason, a purpose, and it is our decision to believe God or not.

Jesus believed in the value of teaching so much that He took three-and-one-half years to train His twelve disciples. Even after devoting all that time, one of them betrayed Him and the others were so afraid after Jesus' death that they hid themselves. But God knew their future wouldn't always be so dismal. After Jesus arose from the dead, He appeared to them, encouraged them, and promised them a gift–the Holy Spirit–for those who would believe and choose to follow. The Holy Spirit would be the glue uniting them together in love and giving them the boldness they needed to do great things for God.

Even though Jesus is perfect, He works with imperfect people. God uses imperfect people to fulfill His perfect plan. He uses our failures and triumphs to teach others of God's grace and goodness. God is a God of patience, love, and integrity. If we follow His lead, we will ultimately become like Him.

****

Growing up on my parents' New Jersey farm was a lot of fun. Each year in the late summer at harvest time the straw piled up on the second floor of our big red barn. I utilized it to build forts and tunnels, creating a maze in which I played for hours at a time. I pretended I was at war and spent hours building fortified positions in order to defend myself against a secret enemy. Never did I see the enemy, but it was fun crawling through man-made tunnels and secret "caves" of straw to be the victor in an imaginary war against an invented enemy.

My parents were not rich in money, but in devotion to God and the church. Each Sunday we faithfully attended the local church, honoring God with all our hearts. I remember learning songs like "Jesus Loves Me" and "Jesus Loves the Little Children" in Sunday school class. David defeating Goliath with his sling; Samson fighting the Philistines with a jawbone; and Elijah calling fire down from heaven were some of my favorite stories from the Bible. I have only fond memories of church as a boy.

One day my mother showed me the way to salvation. She explained who Jesus was and what He did for me by dying on the cross. She spoke to me about sin and how Jesus would forgive me if I asked Him. So at age six at my mother's knee, she guided me in the sinner's prayer and I accepted Jesus as my Savior.

Although I very much love my brother, who is six years younger than I am, I did not always show it when I was young. I loved feeling powerful, yet realistically I did have the advantage. We spent many hours playing Monopoly, Chess, and Risk. Fueled by competitiveness, our imagination influenced our games, such as the "big business" version of Monopoly in which we dealt with millions of dollars, multiple hotels on each property and bank loans. We fulfilled a fantasy of being rich and powerful. Sometimes, as many kids do, we wrestled for fun and I introduced him to Mr. "Charlie Horse." Through him, I learned determination and creativity.

My sister was quite active in her school and enjoyed various sports, especially cheerleading. She practiced cheerleading moves on the kitchen floor. She and I are opposites: she was popular, involved, and responsible, while I was a loner and into trouble. She has always been compassionate and desired good things of other people. I am amazed at how my sister has demonstrated great love, compassion, and integrity over the years.

One of the many great memories I have of my mother is her study of God's Word and the importance she placed on it. My mother is a very intelligent woman. She has taught Sunday school, been a youth pastor, sold real estate, and was determined to served God to the best of her ability. She instilled in her children the importance of the Bible as the very Word of God. I remember one summer she created a chart for my sister, brother and me to record our achievements in Bible reading and Bible memorization in order to receive a prize. Although I do not remember the prize, I do remember the importance she placed on the study of the Holy Scriptures. Even though in Sunday school class I was required to memorize a verse each week, I remember the impact of this simple contest on my life. The most significant memories are the many nights she spent reading and studying the sacred book.

My father has always been a hard worker. I remember the "fun" I had with my father, chopping wood on Saturdays in the late summer and early autumn. We prepared for the winter by cutting down trees, splitting logs, and stacking wood in the basement to heat our home with a wood-burning stove.

My father also taught me to fish at a pond on his farm. He set me up with pole and bait and then left me alone. Out of about a dozen times, there was only one time I experience the thrill of catching some fish. I found a spot where the fish were biting and got so excited about my first catch that I ran to tell my father. He decided it would be a good lesson for me to go through the entire fishing experience by cleaning, gutting, and cooking my two fish. The finished product was less than pleasurable with burned, somewhat scaly fish.

On another occasion, he taught me the proper way to shoot a shotgun. I was very surprised when the power of the explosion sent me backwards a foot or two. I missed the target, but he patiently worked with me to fire the weapon again.

My father is also a quiet man and doesn't speak very much, but when he speaks, it is important to listen. Through him, I learned patience and simplicity in life.

CHAPTER 2

Seeds of Rebellion

For rebellion is as the sin of witchcraft, and stubbornness is as iniquity and idolatry.
1 Samuel 15:23

The prophet Samuel anointed Saul to be the first king of Israel. Saul was a humble man when he was young. The Bible says he was little in his own sight (1 Samuel 15:17) and was actually afraid to become king (1 Samuel 1:21-22). Yet, God chose Saul to be the first king of Israel. The responsibility was great, and at first, Saul did all that he was supposed to do. However, once he became comfortable with his new position, pride and rebellion began to grow in his heart and he began to compromise. As self-importance grew, one time Saul took it upon himself to offer the sacrifice, fulfilling a role he was not called to do, because the prophet Samuel was delayed. As a result, Saul was told his kingdom would not be established. A short time later, God told Saul to totally wipe out the Amalekites. Again, King Saul disobeyed which resulted in the loss of the kingdom promised to his descendants, and God chose another who sought Him.

Rebellion is as the sin of witchcraft because of

improper trust and dependency. Witchcraft is the practice of depending on demonic beings or self rather than Jesus Christ for power. Rebellion is a renunciation of proper authority to which one owes allegiance. To be rebellious means you are fighting against God and depending on your own ability. If you will note, Saul was a believer at first. He believed in Jehovah God, but God later rejected him because of his rebellion and dependency on self. God places a higher standard on those whom He calls. Later, in the last days of his life, Saul consorted with a witch and was told he and his sons would die together in battle. That is the end result of rebellion. The wages of sin is death (Romans 6:23)

****

My mother tells stories of my adventures as a child learning independence. One day my father brought home a pickup truck full of bread meant for cow feed. Along with the bread, there were some cakes, which he placed in the garage refrigerator to keep them cool and away from us kids. I wanted to eat some because I always seemed to be hungry. I remember going into the garage, opening the refrigerator door, and to my amazement seeing boxes of *Hostess* Ding Dongs. I grabbed one and gently opened the aluminum wrapper. As I took my first bite, I was overjoyed at the taste of pure chocolate cake with the sweet smooth cream filling. However, I was not content with just one, so I ate another and then another until I was sick to my stomach.

Eating never seemed to be no problem for me. Another time I went into the cornfield and ate cow corn.

Still another time I ate all the vitamins in my grandmother's cabinet. Many times when mother wasn't looking, I would help myself to my sister's bottle. I learned young in life that if I wanted something, I just had to take it.

At times as a boy, I was mischievous as well. One day while waiting for the school bus at the end of our long driveway, I threw small rocks at cars as they went by. This was fun to me. On one occasion a car stopped, a man got out of the car and sternly rebuked me for throwing the rocks, which I denied ever doing. I was terrified to death! But he didn't do anything else except scare me.

When I was in first grade, I enjoyed getting attention any way possible. Once I seriously injured a fellow student during recess time to get the attention! I bullied another kid and he didn't take too kindly to my attitude. I picked up a rock about the size of my small hand and threw it at him. It hit him in the head and he was rushed to the hospital. As for me, I won the disagreement but had to spend the next week in detention writing "I will not throw rocks."

While growing up, elementary school was uninteresting for me. I was always bored stiff and looked for excitement. Education never interested me when I was young. To feel important, I looked for avenues to create thrill and dumbfound people. I remember the principal's first name because I was a frequent guest in his office. I got into fights weekly; I pulled up girls' dresses; I threw soybeans from the field next to the school at passersby; and I used vulgar language. I lied often and thought only of myself.

One wintry day my parents allowed me to go outside to play in the snow. They told me to come home when the streetlights came on. I didn't listen to them. When I finally did get home, I made up some lie that didn't convince them I was innocent. I was grounded and again got to practice my penmanship by writing, "I promise that I will always come in when the street lights come on" some one-thousand times. It was as if I was consumed with selfishness. I did what I wanted and didn't care about anybody else. That was my life during the week. However, on Sundays, I was a saint.

In my early elementary years, I had many friends in my neighborhood. Most of them I used and abused. They were not really friends, but pawns. I loved racing my bike around the block and playing kickball. I was usually pretty good at kick ball. I could kick the ball farther than any of my teammates and was usually the first to be picked for a team.

I remember only having one serious rival in fifth grade. He was a muscular black boy whom I thought could actually beat me in a fight. So I never picked a fight with him because of my fear of defeat. However, that did not stop me from intimidating other young boys into making them do what I wanted them to do.

In fifth grade, I dared a so-called friend to address the teacher by his first name. He did as I commanded and got into big trouble. I sat back and laughed to myself. I was a selfish brat, seeking my own glory, thrill, and satisfaction, not realizing these young boys and girls I was in class with were actually human beings with feelings and probably went to their parents crying because of my egotism and rebellion. My troublesome ways finally caught up with me and I received suspension from school.

When I was about 9 or 10 years old, my father started teaching me how to plow and disk the fields. It felt commanding to drive the big forty-twenty and twenty-twenty tractors. It made me feel important and my work was so vital to my father that he would actually pay me ten cents an hour to work the fields and drive tractors. However, rebellion was already grounded in me. Many times when I would go to the fields, my father would say to drive through the fields and not on the road because I was still a child and didn't have a license. Whenever I could get away with it, I drove on the smoother road, not only to avoid the bumpy fields, but also to experience the thrill of speed.

I rebelled against authority and anyone who didn't do things my way. I wanted to be the center of my life, and I wanted to do what I wanted to do, regardless of the consequences; regardless of my image; regardless of what my parents wanted. Rebellion does that to a person. Rebellion is resistance or defiance to authority. Rebellion is what got Satan kicked out of heaven. He sought power and self-glory and fulfillment in self rather than in God for whom he was created to serve and worship. I was greatly influenced not by God, but my own selfish desires. Like the Pharisees in the time of Christ, I thought I was living for God because of my religious involvement, but instead I was living for myself.

Religion was the one thing in which I excelled.

Part of it was because I had Christian parents who lived what they believed. Part of it was that in church I felt loved and accepted. I was good at Bible memorization and sword drills. I learned the Bible stories and impressed people with my biblical knowledge. It seemed that God had given me a special understanding of His Word. I felt empowered and recognized for my efforts. However, the life I lived on Sunday was the opposite of the life I lived the rest of the week.

CHAPTER 3

Lessons

Truly God is good to Israel, even to such as are of a clean heart.
Psalms 73:1

In the book of Acts there is a story of a man who was lame from his mother's womb and was carried daily to the gate of the temple to beg for alms (see Acts 3-4). He was 40 years old and had done this all of his life. One day, as Peter and John were on their way to the temple to pray, they saw the man and looked directly at him. Peter then told the man to look at them. The man was expecting to receive something from them, but what they offered was far greater than anything money could buy. Peter said, "Silver and gold have I none; but such as I have give I thee: In the name of Jesus Christ of Nazareth rise up and walk." Then he took him by the right hand, and lifted him up: and immediately his feet and ankle bones received strength" (Acts 3:6, 7). And the man began walking and leaping and praising God!

What I find interesting about this true story is not that the lame man was healed, but that Jesus didn't heal him when He was ministering on earth. Each year Jesus would have seen the man when He went to the temple to participate in the festivals. Why didn't Jesus heal him then? Was He not a compassionate God? I believe the reason was timing. God desires us to wait on Him, to trust in Him, to depend on Him for everything. If God did everything for us in one setting, then our faith in Him would be stunted. Peter and James would have most likely seen this lame man during their visits to the temple with Jesus. Perhaps their hearts were touched, perhaps they even asked Jesus to do something; but whatever the reason, God did eventually answer their prayers at the right time.

****

When I was a little older, we moved away from the farm, and I was introduced to another way of life. We moved into a large house in the central part of New Jersey. By attending another school, I received a fresh start, considering the things I had done at my other school had marred my reputation. At first, I still craved attention, got in a few fights, and angered some people, but then I started to mellow out and become more subdued. I tried to do my best by paying attention in school and doing what my parents desired. It was at this time that church started to appeal to me more. I began to see its importance and showed a little more respect for the things of God. When I was 12 years old I received baptism by water as commanded by Jesus in the gospels. This placed me down the right path. I became more involved in church activities and started really reading my Bible. Good works are what we were created for, but good works never establish righteousness. Only faith in the finished work of Christ brings righteousness.

God is good. He sees the heart of man, while man looks on the outward appearance. Even though I was not perfect, God saw the sincerity of my heart. He knew I wanted to serve Him with all my strength. I am sure there are many people in this world who are sincere but with God that really isn't enough. A person can be sincerely wrong just as easily as he can be earnestly right. A person can hope in himself, just as he can hope in God. A person can love himself more than he loves God, yet think he loves God more than he loves himself. At this stage of my life, I made a determination to serve God. I wanted to do my best to please Him. I wanted to do that which was true. However, I was missing a vital element.

One time at church youth camp, which in my opinion was an annual weeklong camping adventure independent of parents, I prayed a specific prayer to God. A banquet was scheduled at the end of the week to which young men could invite a date. I had never had a date. I asked God for a specific girl. I told Him I wanted a girl with long straight brown hair, about my height, blue eyes, and a figure that met my specifications. Not only was there one person on the entire campground that fit that description–there was two–twins! So I asked one of the twin girls out. She said no, so I asked the other girl out. She said she had another date, so it didn't work out the way I had wanted.

What was the lesson? God can give you what you want, but it may not be what He wants. God has a plan for everyone. We don't always understand it, but He gives us what we need at the perfect time.

Sometimes God brings us through difficult times of frustration, temptation, and struggles to bring us to the point where we realize we need Him. We require His grace and we require His love. We must make it to Golgotha–the place of the skull, the position of death–and I was not there yet. I was climbing the mountain of self, pride, and arrogance. I was full of ego, self-importance, and conceit; and this was the more dangerous mountain to climb with more cliffs and falling rocks and less support.

CHAPTER 4

Power

...and the Lord remembered her
1 Samuel 1:19

In the days before the kings of Israel, there was a woman named Hannah who had a problem only God could solve. She could not bear children. This was a bitter experience for her because in the culture of that day to not be able to bear a son was a great disgrace.

Now Hannah's husband, Elkanah, loved her very much and told her of his love for her, but it was of no comfort to her. She went to the temple of the Lord and made a vow to God saying that if He would answer her prayer and give her a son, she would give him to the Lord all the days of his life. She sought the miraculous; she sought God's blessing; and the Lord remembered her and gave her the son of her desires. She committed him to the Lord, and the young boy became one of the most important prophets of old–establishing kingdoms and turning a people back to God. Samuel had such a relationship with God that God spoke with him on a regular basis. The leadership of Israel was so ungodly they were no longer effective. The Word of the Lord was precious in those days (1 Samuel 3:1) meaning that only on rare occasions did God speak to His people. But Samuel had a pure heart before God, and even as a child, God spoke to him plainly.

God equips His children with everything they need to be effective in the work He has called them to do. God knows what we need, when we need it, and He leads us to the right position to receive it.

****

Overall, my childhood would probably be considered as normal as anyone else's, but it wasn't long before God would do something so incredible to me and for me that up to this day I have never experienced anything quite like it. During a Sunday night church service, November 18 1979, I was sitting with my family on the fourth pew from the front on the right side of an Assembly of God church. I couldn't tell you what the pastor preached because I was daydreaming about going out for ice cream after the service and, therefore, desired the service to get over quickly. Little did I know at the time that my mother had been fasting all week and had made a request to God. As the message ended, the pastor asked, "Is there anyone here who would like to receive the baptism in the Holy Spirit with the evidence of speaking in tongues?" I perked up. This was new to me. I had never considered the question. I had made a commitment to serve Jesus Christ early in life and had been baptized in water. So after giving it a brief thought, I said to myself, "Sure, why not." I went to the altar near the piano, which was to my left. I knew the pastor usually started from that side of the altar when praying for each individual. My father also went up to the altar, but he went to the other side toward the organ. I closed my eyes and asked God to forgive me of my sins. The thought was that God wasn't going to give me the precious gift of the Holy Spirit infilling unless I was in right standing with Him. Then I raised my hands and began to worship God. The pastor prayed for me and continued down the line. I continued to praise God. Then I felt a great power come over me, fell backwards on to the floor, and began to loudly speak in an unknown, unlearned language. I received the baptism in the Holy Spirit that night and everyone knew it. This was marvelous to me, but what was even greater to me was the love I felt. As I lay on the ground with my hands lifted up totally yielded to God while speaking loudly in an unknown tongue, God showed me a little of His love in my heart. For the first time I felt genuine love, a peaceful love, that I cannot adequately explain to this day. This love was authentic, bona fide, unexplainable, and so real that I had no doubt it was the love God had for me. All I could do was cry tears of joy. I have never experienced a love so great, yet so tender, in my entire life. No person could have demonstrated this love to me–only the One who is the purity of Love, God Himself. This is what I had been longing for all my life. But little did I know this was just a small taste of what God had for me. My future would be changed forever, and tribulation would be right beside it. That same night, my father also received the baptism in the Holy Spirit quietly and softly. My mother's prayer was answered.

CHAPTER 5

Simple Faith

Launch out into the deep, and let down your nets for a drought.
Luke 5:4

Simon Peter and his buddies had been fishing all night and had caught nothing. This can be very disappointing for a man that earns his livelihood from fishing. When Jesus saw Peter, He asked, "May I use your boat to give some space so I can teach the people." Peter submitted. After the teaching was over, Jesus told Peter to go out into the deep again so they could "let down his nets for a draught" (Luke 5:4). In the original language, a draught means a haul of fish; not just a large amount, but abundance. The only time *draught* it is used in the Bible is in this passage. Peter was an experienced fisherman. He did this for a living, and every fisherman knows you don't fish in the middle of the day. However, he had learned to trust in Jesus enough to do what He requested and so he took his boats out into the deep. Once they reached the destination, Peter threw the net over the side of the boat and suddenly a great multitude of fishes began to fill the net–so much so that they called their partners over to help so the nets wouldn't completely break from the strain.

What I find interesting is Peter's response to this miracle. He obeyed the Lord and the Lord blessed him, but Peter realized through this experience that God was being good to him and he didn't deserve it for Peter said "Depart from me; for I am a sinful man, O Lord" (Luke 5:8). The Apostle Paul puts it this way, "Or despisest thou the riches of his goodness and forbearance and longsuffering; not knowing that the goodness of God leadeth thee to repentance" (Romans 4:2). Realizing our own inadequacy and the dependency we must have on God is vital to an effective ministry. After this confession of Peter to Christ, Jesus told Peter "Fear not; for henceforth thou shalt catch men." (Luke 5:10) Jesus taught us in the lesson of the fishes that when we obey Him and do exactly as He says, we will reap a great harvest.

****

Full of spiritual fervor and opportunity, I sought direction for my life. I continued my involvement in the youth ministry and other activities in the church. I started reading my mother's religious books, and the Bible became more of a pleasure to me. It wasn't long before God spoke to me. During a Sunday evening service I was looking at the wooden cross hanging behind the pulpit as I did quite regularly when the sermon was being preached. God spoke to me as unmistakable as the crystal blue sky is clear. He called me to preach the gospel, and I knew from that day on I would always be a preacher.

I will never forget one Saturday night in early January 1982; I was 16 ½ years old and in tenth grade; when God gave me a challenge. "Go and witness to the people in your high school." Actually, God gave me this clear and direct command which I did not want to do. "*No way am I going to risk my comfortable life and create enemies by sharing the gospel with people I do not even consider friendly in my high school I thought. Besides, how on earth am I supposed to accomplish this feat anyway? If God wants me to do this then He will have to show me how,*" The next day in Sunday School class, the youth pastor started passing out tracts to each of us, and asked us to pass them out to friends in school. God had heard my prayer.

My high school was made up primarily of three types of people, the - "preps," the "druggies," and the people in the middle. I was in the middle. The "preps" usually came from rich families who could afford the alligator shirts, argyle socks, and polo sweaters. The "druggies" usually wore jeans and t-shirts displaying their favorite heavy metal band. Those in the middle were the ones who was a mix between the two. Although I never did drugs or alcohol, I related more easily to the "druggies" because I thought they seemed more "cool" than the "preps."

My locker was on a corner. Not far from my locker was a hallway that opened to the outside where "druggies" could hang out and smoke before classes started. Because of my fear of witnessing, I made the following plan. I would start passing out tracts to the "druggies" at five-minutes before eight o'clock. When the bell rang at four minutes before eight, the students would leave to go to homeroom and their first class. This would give me the total of one minute to pass out the tracts without any time for confrontation. So when the time came, I followed my plan. For about two weeks, I walked out to the "druggies" and said, "I have something for you," gave them a tract, and kept walking. Some accepted them; some threw them on the ground (when I noticed this, I would pick the tract up and give it back to the person). In my opinion, it was a flawless execution of witnessing. I felt like I had accomplished my task. Eventually, I started actually talking to the "druggies", resulting in some interesting conversations. My confidence started to build. I began bringing my Bible to school and letting others know I was a Christian.

After about two weeks, a student approached me and noticed I was talking about the Lord. He asked if I was a Christian. He had just recently become a Christian, so I invited him to our Friday night youth group. The church was close to the school and I thought he would like it. He agreed to attend and asked if he could bring a few friends. I had no objection to him inviting friends. When he arrived, he and his friends doubled the size of our little youth group. I introduced them as my friends from the school and before long our diminutive youth group of six was growing rapidly. This encouraged my faith greatly. I asked the Lord for fifty souls to be saved by the end of the school year. Later in the spring, we showed the movie *The Cross and the Switchblade* and over one hundred teens attended. By the end of the school year, God had answered my prayer and over fifty teens had given their hearts to Jesus.

It is amazing how God intervenes in situations of individual lives. In tenth grade, I had an English teacher, who, although she was not a Christian, kept a Bible on her desk. She enjoyed reading the Bible as poetry and literature, but did not believe in God. Periodically, she would make mention of this in her class. Because she was the teacher and I was a student, I felt if I responded to the fact, my grade might be negatively affected. One day she gave us an assignment to write a short story, read it in front of the entire class, and then the class would discuss it. This was my opportunity to share the gospel. My self-confidence in my faith had grown over the previous few months and I felt the time was right to share the reality of God in people's lives. One of my favorite Christian rock bands was *Resurrection Band* from Chicago, Illinois. I loved the voice of Glenn Kaiser, lead vocalist, and loved the sound of Christian rock 'n roll. On one of their albums, they sang a song called *Benny and Sue*. It spoke of two young people in love with each other who rode down a road on a motorcycle, ignored a warning sign, and died in a terrible accident. The sad part was they did not know God; thus, they faced eternity without God and with the consequences of their actions. I used this story as a template for my own short story. After reading the story in front of the class, the English teacher, who knew I was a Christian, took the opportunity to ask me some questions about Christianity–particularly concerning those who did not have an opportunity to hear the gospel. As I stood in front of the podium, I began to teach what the Word of God says concerning sinners, being born again, and the love of God. I was able to give hope to those in the class for the rest of the class period. The teacher opened the classroom for any student to ask questions concerning the Bible and God. Never did I realize that God alone can open doors that man chooses to shut, and God can use people who do not even believe in Him to open those doors for the advancement of the gospel. Evangelism has always been my heart. I've always wanted to lead people to Jesus–let them know God loves them, has a plan for their life, and can wash away all their sins if they will just ask Him and believe Jesus Christ died for their sins. The seed was planted in that classroom; in that public school; only God knows the fruit that was produced.

One of the first jobs I had as a teenager was cleaning an elementary school. My father was the head custodian during the day, and I worked the evening shift. I liked this arrangement because many times while left alone in the school, I had the opportunity to think and practice my preaching. Sometimes when I finished my work early, I went to the all-purpose room–which served as a cafeteria, gym, and auditorium–and practiced my preaching skills. I pretended I was conducting a church service with many people seated in the room, listening to my sermons on John 3:16 or Romans 3:23. I would have an altar call and lead people to salvation in Jesus Christ. Later in my adult years, I learned that some of the great evangelists of our time in their early years preached to stumps in the woods and imaginary congregations as well.

I wanted to minister more, so with the youth pastor's permission, I started a prayer service before the regular youth service. I was somewhat of a leader in the youth. Others began to follow my example of witnessing at school. Others began noticing me. The adults in the church began calling me "preacher." I was on cloud nine and loved every minute of it.

CHAPTER 6

Self-Righteousness

For I say unto you, that except your righteousness shall exceed the righteousness of the scribes and Pharisees, ye shall in no case enter into the kingdom of heaven.
Matthew 5:20

Jesus tells a parable of a Pharisee and a publican. The Pharisee was full of self-righteousness, praying a "great" prayer with himself–meaning God was not listening. He spoke of the great man he was, living a life that was "untouched" by the wickedness all around him. He spoke of his giving of tithes, fasting, and how he did not even associate with the wicked. He was full of arrogance, pride, and self-righteousness. The publican, on the other hand, was the lowest of the low in that time. He was a tax collector, despised by the religious leadership and by the people. He knew of his sin and pleaded with God for forgiveness and mercy. He was so ashamed that he would not even look up to God when speaking with Him. The Bible says this man was justified before God for his humility and the Pharisee was not because of his pride.

What lesson can we learn: First, just because your religious, doesn't mean you're in good standing with God. Second, God looks at the heart, not on the outward manifestations of good works alone. Thirdly, God detests those who exalt themselves before other men or God, and will judge them accordingly.

The Pharisees in the New Testament had three main characteristics, which I could relate to at this stage of my life. First, they were knowledgeable about the word of God. Second, they were self-righteous and spiritual looking on the outside. Thirdly, they were arrogant and full of pride.

****

This is what I was becoming. This is what I would eventually have to deal with in my life. I did not realize I was becoming a Pharisee at the time, but it is obvious now that I was. I lived on the thrill of ministry, but did not develop my relationship with Jesus. I was doing all the right things with the approval of the church. I enjoyed the benefits of ministry, but did not look to the One who put me there. Every Christian must deal with this great deception of the flesh. Loren Larson, a preacher, once said, "The flesh is the effort of man to live for God." This is what I was doing–trying to live for God by my own efforts. It was only a matter of time before I fell from the height to which I *thought* I had attained. Within eighteen months, I would run away from home.

One year later, things had settled down from the excitement of the transformation in our youth. Certainly, everybody in the church had been affected in some way. Our youth group had developed into a comfortable size of about forty regularly attending teens. At school, everybody knew I was a Christian and I wore the label with pride and confidence. My reputation as a minister was firmly established. My call into the ministry was obvious: so therefore, I was given opportunity to preach and teach.

I will never forget my very first sermon. The youth were in charge of a Sunday night service. The youth pastor had chosen "faith, hope, and love" as topics. I was to speak on *Faith*, someone else on *Hope*, and the youth pastor would finish with *Love*. I prepared in all earnestness, spending hours writing down everything I knew about faith. When I got up to preach, I preached everything I knew about faith in five minutes. But I was comfortable behind of the pulpit and I knew I was called. To this day, I still have the original notes. It seemed my future was bright, and I was preparing to go to Bible college. Anybody could look at me and see my spirituality; but it was all show on the outside. Inside I was dead.

CHAPTER 7

Idolatry

And they left the house of the LORD God of their fathers, and served groves and idols: and wrath came upon Judah and Jerusalem for this their trespass.
2 Chronicles 24:18

The second of the Ten Commandments found in Exodus 20 specifically speaks to the making of graven images. God did not give requests or recommendations, but commands; and He expects them to be obeyed without question. The apostle John tells us to "keep yourselves from idols" (1 John 5:21). What does it mean be an idol worshiper? What is an idol? Does this apply to our lives today?

In the times of early Israel, the children of God were surrounded by many false religions. In honor of those religions, man created works of stone and wood to represent its deities. It was not uncommon to bow down and worship these works of art that represented their gods. When God called Israel out of Egypt and miraculously delivered them from their enemies, He made it quite clear that He would not share His glory with another deity. The first of the Ten Commandments was to have no other gods before the one true God. Since God is Spirit, there is not an image to create. God did not want Israel to worship a stone, but to worship in Spirit and in Truth (see John 4:23-24).

Today, most of us do not create a statue made of stone or wood then bow down and worship it. However, we can let things become idols. The purpose of an idol is to worship something we can see. We can make an idol of anything we place before God such as materialism, money, lust for power, religious titles, religious activity, and the list is unending. God requires our all–nothing less and nothing added. He requires complete surrender of anything that hinders our relationship with Him. Complete obedience. Anything that keeps us from that intimacy can be an idol from which we must rid ourselves. In Old Testament times the law required only that no graven image be made. Now God requires me to look deep into my heart and see what idols of pride I am holding onto and to surrender them to Him.

****

At this time I had no life of Christ in me. I just went through the motions of fulfilling my religious obligations, rituals, traditions, and keeping all the rules so I looked spiritual on the outside. I thought I was okay because this is all I knew. But inside I was like a rotting log–decaying, disintegrating, and falling apart. I was hollow. There was no depth to my spiritual experiences. It was primarily an act. I did not understand love, not genuine love. Either I had never seen it very clearly in any one person or the church, or I was so ignorant and full of self that I couldn't see it. Either way, it was a hard road and at times I felt just burned out. However, how could I be burned out when I was doing all the right spiritual things? When I was doing everything I had been told to do?

The double life I lived escalated rapidly. During this time, I was into Christian music–I really loved to listen to Christian music. I coveted Christian music; however, I didn't have much money. I found a bookstore that had once been a house with separate rooms for books, music, and gifts and I devised a way to steal the music I wanted. I stole over one hundred cassettes of my favorite music within a short period of time. I even stole some money for concert tickets–although I never went to the concert for fear of being caught, I kept the money. My confidence grew in thievery so if I wanted something, I just stole it. Many times I stole my father's pickup truck to commit my crimes. The ironic thing is that the Christian music didn't have any spiritual effect on me. I listened to it for two reasons: 1) I liked the music, and 2) Christians weren't supposed to listen to secular music. I hid my growing collection of music under my bed. Again, I was unintentionally training as a Pharisee. About a year later, my parents began asking questions, took virtually all of my cassettes away, and threw them in a dumpster.

I coveted. The Bible says covetousness is the same as idolatry (see Colossians 3:5). I was setting up the idol of Christian music. I loved Christian music so much that I had to have it. Now, how can Christian music be an idol when it is supposed to glorify God? Anything we put before God can be an idol. Covetousness is a trademark of a Pharisee and I was becoming the chief of all Pharisees.

In the summer of 1983, when I was a few months shy of eighteen, my neighbor hired me part-time to do some yard work. The job provided gas money for my 1967 multi-colored, rusty, Volkswagen beetle. One day, he paid me in advance by check and left me alone to finish the work. Before he left, I asked to use the restroom, which gave me the opportunity to leave the window cracked so I could enter the house after he left. I walked through the house going through personal things–looking for anything of value I could take and not look suspicious. I found a walkman and a book of blank checks–a gold mine of financial treasures. Within a few days I had practiced his signature enough to forge it on a blank check. The first check I wrote was for a low amount. I thought I could say it was just a regular paycheck and nothing would look dubious. Once I cashed the first check without incident, I wrote another for a larger amount, then another for three hundred dollars. In total, I ended up stealing about seven hundred dollars in forged checks. I had no conscience and didn't consider being caught. I tried to be careful in what I bought, because I didn't want my parents to find out. I spent most of it on food, arcade games, and trips to the beach while playing hooky from school. I also discovered the adult movie theater.

CHAPTER 8

Fear

But if we shall say, of men; we fear the people;
for all hold John as a prophet.
Matthew 21:26

The religious leaders of Jesus' time were driven by fear. They feared Jesus so they sought to have Him killed. (Matthew 26:4, John 7:1, 25) They were afraid of Lazarus, whose only crime was rising from the dead, for they thought they would lose their influence over the people (John 12:10). They also feared the people because they couldn't explain the beheading of John the Baptist who preached repentance, and the people thought he was a prophet. (Matthew 21:27) Any time people are in power, they must deal with the problem of fear. When you have money, position, power, you can lose it. That's why God commands us not to love the things of this world for they will all pass away (1 John 2:15-17). And that's why it is harder for the rich to inherit the kingdom of God than the poor (Matthew 19:23). The poor realize their need; the rich usually do not.

There is no fear in love. Perfect love comes from God. If a person is living in fear, he is not living in love or "in Christ." Some people worry because of fear. First

Timothy 6:10 says, "The love of money is the root of all evil." Most evil leads to fear. Think about it. You desire more money so you can have a good education because if you don't, you fear you won't have the lifestyle you desire. Some fear they will not have enough emergency supplies in case of a catastrophe or enough investments so they can retire with ease. There is nothing wrong with preparing because the Bible teaches that; but when it controls you, it leads to fear. Fear torments. That is not of God. The Christian allows the love of God to cast out all fear (see 1 John 4:18). Fear also blinds us to true love.

****

A musical that our youth presented, *Hello Paul*, was the story of the life of Paul the apostle. I played the lead role of the apostle. I enjoyed participating in the musical dramas we did quite often during my teenage years. However, I was in a dilemma. The fear of being caught for the forged checks began to haunt me. I had to figure out a way to get out of the mess I created. I decided to run away from home. I still had about four hundred dollars of the money I had stolen, and so I chose to go to Chicago. There were two primary reasons I chose Chicago: (1) my favorite Christian Rock band lived there, and (2) there was a shelter for people in need. I thought I could live at the shelter for a while until I found a job and was able to support myself. The only dilemma now was waiting for the right opportunity to leave.

I told my best friend where I was going. No one else knew or even had a clue. I had my plan: I would participate in the *Hello Paul* musical on Sunday, because I couldn't let my church down (how double-minded!). Then, play sick from school on Tuesday because that was the day my mother would be at the church prayer meeting, and my father would be at work, so I would be alone. All went as planned. Tuesday morning after my mother left, I took the suitcase I had packed the night before, got in my car, and left home. I placed a note with the dishes explaining why I was running away. I thought they would find the note at dinner. (As it turned out, nobody saw the note because after my trip was discovered, they ordered out and didn't cook at home). As I was leaving, I stopped at a red light and my father pulled up to the intersection at the same time. I was surprised and wondered if he would follow me. He did not and I continued my route to Chicago. It began to snow.

Before I went too far, I wanted a little more money so I forged another check for a little over one thousand dollars. When I went through the drive-thru at the bank, they said I had to cash it inside and that scared me. So I said I would be right in, but instead kept on driving into the center of the snowstorm.

I listened to Christian music most of the way. I still considered myself a Christian. I thought I was doing what was best and had no conscience of any sin I had committed. One artist and one song I listened to a lot while driving to Chicago was a song sung by the group *Kansas* on their *Vinyl Confessions* album–one of the few Christian albums they produced–called, "Play the Game Tonight." The chorus goes like this:

Play, play the game tonight
Can you tell me if it's wrong or right?
Is it worth the time, is it worth the price
Do you see yourself in the white spotlight?
Then play the game tonight

This song is about an artist playing at a concert, but for me it had a spiritual significance. Without really realizing it, I was playing a game with God, church and my spirituality. I was playing a game. My heart was hard, and my selfishness was established front and center.

After a few hours the snow was beginning to accumulate, so I found a motel to spend the night. It took me about two and a half days to make the trip to Chicago.

When I arrived, I found the shelter, JPUSA, which stands for Jesus People USA and I went into the foyer. I said to the receptionist, "Hello, my name is Jeff Wooden and I need a place to stay."

"What is your name?" The lady asked.

"I am Jeff Wooden."

"Oh…your mother called. She wants you to call her back!"

I was shocked! *How did she find out? I had left everything behind, how did she know exactly where I would be three days later?* I thought. Then, I started to cry. The receptionist pointed to a phone where I could call out collect. I picked up the phone, called, and explained the main details of what I had done. They informed me my best friend had told them. They asked and I agreed to return home.

The next day I began my drive back to New

Jersey. My parents wanted me to call them every few hours. When I was near Toledo, Ohio, my car started having problems. They agreed to drive all the way out to Toledo to help me back home. They left with my brother and sister early the next morning, Saturday, and drove to Toledo. They arrived late Saturday night. I was playing an arcade game when they arrived. I asked them to wait a minute while I finished the game. My selfishness! They had driven over five hundred miles to get me–sacrificing their weekend–and *I asked them to wait a minute because I was playing an arcade game*! I was so arrogant.

CHAPTER 9

Pride

The pride of thine heart hath deceived thee.
Obadiah 1:3

The nation of Edom was a close neighbor of Israel in the age of the kings. They were in close friendship with Israel. Yet, Obadiah tells us they did not help Israel when they were in need. Instead they desired the material things Israel had and took advantage of Israel's weakened state (Obadiah 1:9, 13). The Lord gave Obadiah a vision that they would be brought down because of the pride of their hearts. They were proud of their secured position of habitation in the cliffs and confident in their own strength, but God brought them down low (1:3-4). They were proud of their wealth, but God made them poor; their wealth taken away by force (1:5-6). Their diplomats were deceived (1:7), their wise men destroyed (1:8), and their mighty warriors cut off by slaughter (1:9). This was a strong nation; yet, God destroyed this nation because of their pride.

Leviticus 26:19 tells us that God "will break the pride of your power" speaking of His people who despise God statues, detest God's judgments, do not obey all of God commandments, and break His covenant or disown

Him. (Leviticus 26:15) History tells us that God keeps His part of the bargain.

Pride is the greatest sin a man can have. The lust of the eyes, the lust of the flesh, and the pride of life all have their foundation in pride. Satan fell from heaven because of pride. Adam and Eve fell into sin because of pride. It is the exact opposite of complete trust and dependency upon Jesus Christ. It exalts self instead of Jesus, and one cannot be a believer unless pride is rooted out.

****

The next day we left early to make the trip back to New Jersey. If possible, we wanted to make it to Sunday night church. I looked forward to this because I assumed I would be welcomed back like the prodigal son. I looked forward to a "great reception" of my "celebrated return." True, things needed to be resolved, but "I was returning!" We returned in time for the service, but I did not get the greeting I thought I deserved; instead, I was denounced and stripped of all involvement in any future church leadership activities. I was allowed only one thing–attend church. I was not even allowed be an usher. I had embarrassed my family, my church, and my friends. Nothing would ever be the same again.

My parents repaid the man from whom I had stolen the money, and I agreed never to go near him or his family again. He dropped the charges. My parents were dumbfounded as to how their son could do such a thing. Simply put, I was just doing what I wanted to do without consideration for anyone else. Looking back, I believe I was acting like the religious people in the church on the outside, but I hadn't comprehended or understood the intimate relationship they had with Jesus on the inside. I was self-righteous, arrogant, prideful, selfish, and not living like a genuine Christian.

The next couple of years were humbling to me. I concentrated on finishing high school and saving money for Bible college. I still had the call of God on my life, but my opportunities for ministry were practically non-existent. I participated in a few coffeehouse ministries that other churches sponsored. That was limited, but God was merciful. During this time, I had the opportunity to explain to a young man the importance of the baptism in the Holy Spirit with the evidence of speaking in tongues. He sought and was filled. I still felt useful to God.

In the Bible Jonah is an excellent example of how a person may be called of God for a specific purpose; yet, due to his own arrogance and pride, he rebels against God and God has to discipline him. In the case of Jonah, he was thrown overboard and swallowed by a fish while running in the opposite direction of where God wanted him to go. God provided a means for Jonah to get to his destination–the fish; but Jonah still had to be obedient and preach to the people he despised. It isn't always easy to obey God, especially when we have to be humbled. Nevertheless, God is full of grace and mercy; He is gentle like a good Shepherd leading His sheep.

After a brief time at a Bible institute in New York, I was accepted to Central Bible College in Springfield, Missouri. I craved the opportunity to get away from home and be independent. I started in the fall of 1985 and enjoyed my independence as much as I could. Professionally, I felt I was doing the right thing; after all, I thought ministers are supposed to have a Bible education. However, in reality, I never put any serious effort into studying. I excelled in acting spiritual, and I looked the part of a minister on the outside, but I still had torrents of self-righteousness and pride rushing out of me like the gushing geyser *Old Faithful* at Yellowstone National Park. At one time my entire dorm room was filled with posters of my favorite Christian rock bands. I got tired of them, so I turned them over, wrote scripture verses on them with black marker, and re-hung them on the walls. When entering my room, you saw the walls full of scriptures. My intent was to use this technique as a tool for memorization, but in my heart I thought it made me look spiritual. I knew I needed an intimate relationship with Jesus and told everyone I had one, but it was a one-way relationship of which I had no part. It wasn't long before this artificial relationship was reflected in my schoolwork. Bible classes were easy for me since I had grown up in Sunday school, but the general education was uninteresting to me. As a result, I lost my student loan money after three semesters due to my low grades.

****

Although illegal drugs, alcohol, and cigarettes have not been an issue with me, in my late teens I began to lust after women. This was my weakness. Pornography is a secret sin. One can participate in this sin without others knowing. It grows like a cancer in the mind. The simplest picture can distract you. The simplest thought can control you. And for me it became the culmination of my selfishness–I wanted it, so I pursued it. I started to pursue this sin aggressively while I was in Bible college (ironic isn't it!). I was independent, self-supporting–with the government's help–and most of all, I was able to do what I wanted. My life was extremely self-absorbed during this time. I had some, but not very many friends, including girl friends. I wanted sex, so I located a prostitute and lost my virginity–a fact of which I am not proud. Sometimes God has to get us to the point of desperation before He can deliver us. We have to get to the place of humility.

"A broken and a contrite heart, O God, thou wilt not despise" (Psalms 51:17). Very few Pharisees in the Bible followed Jesus before Pentecost. There are all kinds of examples of people trying to make it on their own in the Bible–Jacob, Samson, and the Israelites–before they would cry out to God in desperation for help. This is what God had to do for me. However, it would be another ten years before I realized that I really needed God. You see at this time, I was a Christian of convenience–as long as it served me, I would continue in the religious activity

What is pride? What is selfishness? What does it mean to be so self-centered, self-absorbed, and self righteous that only a miracle can transform you into a man of humility and meekness? The easiest way to understand pride is to look at the word and notice the center letter in the word *pride*. It is *I*. *I* is really the foundation of sin. Pride is what caused Satan to fall from

God's service in heaven. Pride deals with self; pride is absorbed with me; and pride exalts everything that is contrary to godliness. When self is put first, you can be assured that pride is the center of this wrongdoing. I heard a preacher on the radio once say, "We don't deny sin, but we deny self." This is a difficult lesson for most people to learn, and it was especially difficult for me.

INTERLUDE

The war had hardened my heart and resolve. I was determined to win this battle no matter what the cost. The enemy had been relentless–constantly attacking; constantly bombarding; constantly demoralizing. This enemy was always near, always cunning, always quiet–attacking subtly and unsuspectingly. It seemed the enemy was more powerful and I was outnumbered, outgunned, and surrounded. A few times I had small victories, but defeat was more common. I had struggled for so long that I didn't know any other life. It was never-ending. Every time I gained some ground, it wouldn't be long before the enemy would get it back. When the enemy gained the upper hand, I would figure out a way to regain the lost territory, but never enough to totally overcome him.

Now I lay buried in a small cavern surrounded by rock on all sides. The only entry was blocked so the enemy couldn't find me. I had dug myself into a pit and didn't know how to get out. Would this war ever end? Would I ever be victorious? How would I defeat this foe? How could I get rid of this enemy once and for all? Would there ever be peace?

CHAPTER 10

Into the Wilderness

But God led the people about, through the way of the wilderness.
Exodus 13:18

In each of the synoptic gospels' records, we see Jesus, after being baptized by John being compelled by the Holy Spirit to go into the wilderness to be tempted by the devil. The gospel of Mark tells us that he was "driven" or "ejected" out of his comfort zone and placed in this land of dry barrenness. The wilderness is not only a place of dry barrenness, but, a place of loneliness, heat, and wild animals. There is little vegetation, little shelter, and little comfort.

Historically, the wilderness has been a place where people have had their greatest revelations of God. Paul spent three years in the wilderness being taught by Jesus (Galatians 1:17-18). The Israelites spent forty years in the wilderness learning the law of God given to them by God thru Moses who spoke with God on a regular basis. The Israelites also saw the miraculous provision of a mighty God for those forty years. It was also in the wilderness that Moses saw the burning bush and was called by God to lead Israel out of bondage.

The wilderness can be a place of great struggle or a place of encouragement. It can also be a place of desperation where the call of God on one's life needs to be assured.

****

After leaving Bible college, due to poor grades, I moved to Florida where my family resided. I questioned my calling, pursued my fleshly appetites, and wandered like a man in search of purpose. I actively pursued the immoral lifestyle of prostitutes, strip bars, and adult video arcades. I did things that are shameful to talk about and ungodly, to say the least. There is a saying that if you have two dogs of equal strength, size, and breed, the one you feed the most will be the stronger one. In my frustration over my life, I succumbed to my own desires and fed that which was ungodly, immoral, and sinful. At one time, I even had a job at a convenience store that sold porn. My mind was darkened with the wickedness of sinful thoughts and attitudes. I sought ways to satisfy my fleshly, sinful appetites. I was self-centered and absorbed in this world of sin. I knew it was wrong, but my flesh craved it and the Holy Spirit fire was quenched.

My relationship with Christ suffered. I still went to church and put on the religious coat of deception, but in my heart, I did what I wanted. I believed that I had mastered this deception very well. In my own mind, I convinced myself of anything I wanted. I still taught Sunday School and was involved in the leadership of the youth. Some who were sensitive to the Holy Spirit may have known things I dealt with, but it seemed to me that

I had the best of both worlds–secretly living in sin and involved in ministry. However, this addiction did not enhance my relationship with God and inside I was a miserable wreck.

Nevertheless, God had not left me.

During my time in Florida, God spoke directly to me in two distinct dreams. These dreams gave me hope.

In the first dream: *I was like Aaron when Moses anointed him. The oil dripped on my head, in my beard and saturated my clothes. The anointing fell on me and I had power to preach the gospel.*

At the end of the dream, I woke up immediately and prayed to God for mercy.

Less than a week later, I was talking about other issues with the associate pastor in his office. At the end of the counseling session, the pastor paused, got some oil, and anointed me to preach. This was unusual. I had not told him of the dream and we had not talked about ministry or preaching. I believe he fulfilled the part of Moses in the dream. The presence of God came on me. It greatly influenced my life.

Shortly after the first dream God gave me another: *I was a soldier in squad formation. A few brief words were given, than the soldiers were dismissed. All the soldiers were "Christians". At the dismissal, women came and seduced all the other men into sexual sin. I resisted the women and went down a hall. I heard noises in one of the rooms. I looked in several doors before finding a demon-possessed corporal. Another religious man was trying to cast the demon out without success. I was full of the Spirit and rebuked the demon in the name of Jesus. The demon left immediately. I was a little surprised and asked the Lord Jesus how*

I was able to rebuke the devil when the other man couldn't. Jesus said it was because I abstained from sexual immorality and submitted myself to Him. I was given the authority to do this and would be able to do other miraculous things, as well, if I stayed pure and holy to God. The other "soldiers" missed out because of their sexual sins.

At the end of the dream, I woke up immediately and prayed to God for mercy.

The summary of what God was telling me during this wilderness experience of my life was that God had anointed me for ministry and I needed to keep myself sexually pure so He could use me to do miraculous things. This gave me clarity of purpose and confidence in God's call on my life. Now, it was time to go back and finish what I had started.

CHAPTER 11

Misplaced Trust

A man shall not be established by wickedness: but the root of the righteous shall not be moved.
Proverbs 12:3

What is an addict? Webster's Dictionary defines an addict as one "devoted or surrendered to something habitually or excessively." A person can be addicted to sex, drugs, alcohol, coffee, movies, or just about anything. For the Christian, a person becomes an addict when he yields to his own selfish desires and flesh rather than God's desires and the Holy Spirit. This is a higher standard than that of the world. The Bible says, "Walk in the Spirit, and ye shall not fulfill the lust of the flesh. For the flesh lusteth against the Spirit, and the Spirit against the flesh: and these are contrary the one to the other: so that ye cannot do the things that ye would." (Galatians 5:16,17). The works of the flesh are described in the following verses: "Now the works of the flesh are manifest [made plain] which are these; Adultery, fornication (harlotry and incest), uncleanness (impurity, sexual or moral), lasciviousness (looseness, promiscuity), idolatry, witchcraft, hatred (hostility), variance (quarreling), emulations (jealousy and indignation), wrath, strife, seditions (divisive), heresies, envyings, murders (can include murder of character), drunkenness, revellings (partying or riots), and such like: of the which I tell you before, as I have also told you in times past, that they which do such things shall not inherit the kingdom of God" (Galatians 5:19-21). Our flesh constantly struggles against what God wants to do in our lives. We must not yield to it, but we must yield to the promised Holy Spirit, who produces fruit of joy, peace, patience, faithfulness, gentleness, and self-control to name just a few (see Galatians 5:22-23). When a person becomes an addict, he no longer trusts God; he no longer believes God; and the reality is, he is no longer living for God. However, because of God's grace and mercy, we can place our faith in Him and the finished work done at the cross and be free from any addiction "For whom the Son (Jesus) sets free is free indeed" (John 8:36). A preacher once said, "God does not give victory to fallen man. He gives victory to His Son, Jesus Christ". It is not what you do that delivers you; it is Who you trust.

****

Five years after leaving Bible college, I returned with new vigor and resolve. I had a goal and knew this was what God wanted me to do. I studied for my classes and seriously began to pursue the ministry part of my calling. However, the addiction to pornography was not easily silenced in my life.

When I was in college, I rarely pursued relationships with women for marriage because I trusted God would take care of that part. Ironic isn't it? I could trust God to give me a helpmate for life, but I couldn't trust Him with my sexual addiction. I made my requests to God as to the kind of *lady* I desired, but concentrated primarily on my studies. Then one day, I saw her.

One cold January morning as I waited at a bus stop to go to class, she walked toward me. I thought I saw an angel. Her hair with a little red tint to it was shoulder length and she wore a forest green long leather jacket. She had the most beautiful smile and soft, tender eyes. I immediately introduced myself upon her arrival at the bus stop. I was wearing an ugly gray Russian hat I had found at a yard sale for ten cents. Her first impression didn't consider me as possible husband material, but God had other plans. A year and a half later, we were married.

My wife and I remained sexually pure throughout our entire courtship. There were times of temptation and narrow escapes, but we waited until we were married before we united. I knew in my heart that this was the right thing to do. My addiction to pornography was sporadic, but it still controlled me. I needed help. I couldn't overcome on my own, but I didn't know what to do. I had not yet learned the secret that overcoming sin has nothing to do with denying sin.

I secretly carried my addiction of pornography into my marriage. This was not intentional for I thought the struggle would be over once I got married. Although I did not marry my wife to fulfill my lustful cravings, I thought it would make it easier to overcome the addiction. After all, the Apostle Paul says in 1 Corinthians 7:9 that it's better to marry than to burn with lust.

Movies had a special attraction to me rather than magazines or other forms of adult entertainment. I rented movies for the sex scenes; watched them privately when my wife wasn't home; and then thought about them. I never brought any of this into the bedroom for I knew what I was doing was wrong, and I had to look spiritual to my wife. A few times I secretly met with a prostitute simply for selfish reasons. I was in bondage, immersed in sin, captivated to lust, and wanting out but not knowing how. I was also a little confused. I thought if the availability of sex whenever I wanted could not control my addiction, what could? I thought that marriage would be the solution to my sexual addiction. Our marriage was wonderful in many respects. I enjoyed the companionship, the love, and all the other benefits of marriage. I genuinely loved my wife to the best of my ability. I did everything I could to make her happy and the marriage a success. However, living together makes it harder to hide things from each other. I had misplaced my trust in God with trust in marriage. Within the first two years, she started asking questions and I confessed everything to her. Rather than building trust in my marriage, I had destroyed whatever trust there was. She asked me to leave.

CHAPTER 12

Self-Will

So now it is no longer I who do it,
but sin that dwells within me.
Romans 7:17

Paul the apostle struggled with the flesh in his early life as a Christian. "For I know that in me (that is, in my flesh,) dwelleth no good thing: for to will is present with me; but *how* to perform that which is good I find not. For the good that I would I do not: but the evil which I would not, that I do. Now if I do that I would not, it is no more I that do it, but sin that dwelleth in me" (Romans 7:18-20).

The sin nature passed down from Adam and Eve is a part of every man from birth. We see this vividly in the selfishness of little children. Observe two babies in one crib with one toy. Will they naturally share? I think not! Each child tries to keep the toy for himself. They will fight, they will steal, and they will whine and cry until they get their way. Sharing is taught and not a part of the human nature. This is also the problem with man thinking that man is good at heart. The Bible says, "For the imagination of man's heart *is* evil from his youth" (Genesis 8:21).

Self-helps, self-will, self-effort, and self-determination–all emphasized my ability to work out *my* addiction. Nothing that starts with *self* will ever succeed. Any time I am at the center of my solution, I will fail. It is inevitable because God cannot get the glory when I am the answer to my problems, and God will not share His glory. All this started in the Garden of Eden. When Eve was tempted to partake of the fruit so she would become wise, selfishness arose. God had explicitly told Adam not to take from the fruit of the tree of the knowledge of good and evil. Instead of obeying God, they thought about themselves. It is inevitable that when self becomes the center, self becomes the loser. The consequences of their actions lead to spiritual and physical death.

When a man becomes a born-again Christian, his faith becomes focused on what Jesus Christ accomplished on the Cross, i.e. the finished work of Christ. By faith in this finished work all sins are forgiven, the sinner becomes a saint, and he becomes a new creature in Christ (2 Corinthians 5:17). He is justified, that is, declared righteous before God. He is sanctified or made holy in God's sight and he will one day be glorified and receive a new body and spend eternity with Jesus Christ. It is also true that by faith in the finished work, the sin nature becomes dormant or unplugged from its power source in the Christian's life. Of course, just as one must believe in this finished work for salvation, one must also believe in the finished work for deliverance and every other gift that comes from God. (See Colossians 2:6-7.) If one no longer trusts in the finished work, then the sin nature will revive. Until one understands the full impact of what Christ did on the cross of Calvary, man will always struggle with sin and addiction.

****

I had no place to go so I stayed with a friend. The next day I made plans to get my own apartment until we could work out a solution. My wife was devastated. I would have been too if I had been in her position. I loved my wife, but my addiction controlled me so much that it was destroying everything I held dear. I was a double-minded and unstable man. At this time, I was a credentialed minister and expected to be leading by example. I had graduated from Bible college, but my education did not help me; my marriage did not help me; my self-will did not help me; and my prayers were not immediately answered to my satisfaction. I was frustrated, angry, and questioned God as to why I was not delivered–after all I was trying to do God's work. Why wouldn't He help me with this one little addiction? I was at the bottom of an inescapable well of despair with all hope of deliverance gone. Nevertheless, it would only get worse.

My wife asked if I wanted to save our marriage. I said, "Yes, of course." So she set the ground rules and I agreed. The first thing was to remove the VCR and to seek counseling. I wanted deliverance and thought this would help. Although counseling helped us to understand issues such as the differences between men and women a little better; I continued my addiction in secret. During the counseling sessions, which at times I attended alone, the counselor suggested finding an accountability partner. I felt uncomfortable and doubtful of the idea working. A partner cannot always be there and how can I trust in someone who probably is struggling with issues himself. (Later I would learn that the Holy Spirit is a great accountability partner). Next, the counselor suggested I meet with some other men and talk about our experiences. Talking about the addiction all the time only kept my mind on the sin and in some cases glorified the addiction. This didn't work. Another suggested strategy was to stay away from certain parts of town to remove temptation. However when temptation was intensive, I uncaringly went anyway. My self-will and self-determination did not last. People in the church prayed specifically for deliverance giving temporary relief until I was alone and the desires became stronger than my own will to fight. I tried the spiritual approach of more church participation, Bible reading, and prayer. However, the more I prayed about it, the more I thought about it; the more I wanted to give in and sin. One time after I was reading the Bible, I left the house, and went to an adult video arcade just because I wanted to do so. Reading the Bible and prayer only gave me a temporary peace.

I concentrated on self-effort. In Bible college I had learned the importance of psychology in a person's life. Unfortunately, psychology is great at diagnosing sin, but gives no help to overcoming sin on a permanent basis because its foundation is self and self is flawed.

The addiction was sporadic, so God used me in preaching and teaching as a credentialed minister. I led a Sunday school class on evangelism; I ministered at the altar; and I participated in prayer meetings. However, much of my adult life was a reflection of my teenage years of doing the work of religion, hiding my faults, looking spiritual outside but dead inside. Finally by 1997, I could take the hypocrisy no more. I resigned my ministerial credentials and took a sabbatical from ministry. I was tired, worn-out, burned-out, and frustrated. I decided if God was not going to deliver me, I could not and would not serve Him in ministry. I would remain a Christian, but not pursue my calling. Enough was enough!

I wanted deliverance. I had done everything the pastors and counselors had asked with sincerity and determination, but nothing helped beyond a temporary relief. I did not want a temporary deliverance I wanted a genuine permanent deliverance as God performed for the Israelites when they had to press on toward the Promised Land rather than return to Egypt. I needed a miracle, not unlike the ones I had heard about from missionaries who cast out demons, healed the lame, and made the blind see. I determined not to fight anymore. I wanted deliverance or death. If God wouldn't help me, then why was I serving Him?

CHAPTER 13

Sit and Wait

Wait on the LORD: be of good courage, and he shall strengthen thine heart: wait, I say, on the LORD
Psalms 27:14

The prophet Daniel was a man of great integrity and served the Lord with diligence and honor. Many times, he fasted and prayed to God for guidance, deliverance, and understanding. According to Daniel 10:3, he says: "I ate no pleasant bread, neither came flesh nor wine in my mouth, neither did I anoint myself at all, till three whole weeks were fulfilled." He was mourning for his own sins and the sins of his people. Then God answered him, encouraged him, and gave him understanding.

Simeon was a devout and just man at the time of the birth of Christ. He had waited for the consolation of Israel that is, for the coming of the Messiah. The Holy Spirit had said he would not see death until he had seen the Lord's Christ. The Holy Spirit led him to the temple on the particular day when Jesus was dedicated according to Jewish custom. Once he saw the Child Jesus, he blessed God, and was then ready to die in peace. (See Luke 2:29-30). Simeon had waited for God to keep His promise.

To wait on God is not always an easy thing to do. *To wait* is the same concept as a waiter or server in a restaurant. The waiter takes your order then serves you with food and drink in anticipation of receiving a tip. Waiting on God includes an extra step–a binding together. Referring to the example of the waiter in a restaurant, it would include all the things mentioned previously plus taking the time to talk with you, getting to know you, and becoming a close and long-lasting friend to you. For those who wait on God the rewards are immensely desirable. Yes, the rewards of waiting on God are incomparably desirable.

****

This decision took me from the open land of ministry opportunities of a small church to the country of low accountability of a large church of a few thousand people where no one asks if you missed church on Sunday and no one approaches you about getting involved or doing ministry. This was the perfect environment for my sabbatical.

My relationship with God at the time was a wait-and-see approach. Was God going to deliver me? Was He really interested in my deliverance? How was He going to deliver me? I needed answers to these sincere questions. Sometimes I went to church seeking answers to these questions. When attending, I intentionally played the quiet visitor, desiring refreshment from the Word without giving out anything. I did not desire or seek any ministry opportunities and did not receive any.

Sometimes I didn't go to church because I was frustrated at the time it was taking God to answer. However the Bible clearly states, "They that wait upon the LORD shall renew *their* strength; they shall mount up with wings as eagles; they shall run, and not be weary; *and* they shall walk, and not faint" (Isa 40:31). Eventually, I started to wait on Him and one evening He gave me the answer for Victory!

CHAPTER 14

In Christ

As ye have therefore received Christ Jesus the Lord, so walk ye in Him.
Colossians 2:6

Jesus has given the believer unbelievable benefits.

In Romans 6, we see the importance of being baptized into Christ and the benefits of that relationship. Paul tells us in verses 3-5 that when we are baptized into Christ, we are baptized into His death. This means that just as He died, when we place our trust in Him, we die with Him. Moreover, just as death has no dominion over Jesus Christ, so we as Christians have the hope of eternal life. However, it goes farther than just eternal life. This hope we have in Christ also includes abundant life, peace, freedom, and sin not having dominion over us as believers. (See John 10:10b; John 14:27; Galatians 5:1; Romans 6:14).

Let me explain it like this. In order to turn off a lamp, you must turn off the switch. The power for the lamp to work again can be activated by turning on the switch. This is how the sin nature works in the life of a person without God. No matter how hard they try, no matter how much they know better, no matter how much will power they have, it is just way to easy to turn on the switch and sin again and again. This is why the Old Testament law was given. It was to reveal that man could not keep from turning the lamp on and falling back into sin and man's inability to save himself. When Jesus conquered sin at the cross He defeated all the power of sin and unplugged the lamp from the power source. There is no power to turn the lamp on unless you plug it back into the wall, in other words go back to the law. The Christian no longer lives under law but is led by the Holy Spirit. Paul calls it in Romans 8:2 "The Law of the Spirit of life" and according to Galatians 5:18, "If ye be led of the Spirit, ye are not under the law." It is *only* when we leave the cross and try to live by law –or outside of God's way—does our flesh revive and we struggle with sin. The battle lies in the law. Paul puts it this way: "But sin, taking occasion by the commandment, wrought in me all manner of concupiscence (longing for that which was wrong). For without the law sin *was* dead. For I was alive without the law once: but when the commandment came, sin revived, and I died" (Romans 7:8-9). Law is good, but trusting in rules for victory is misplaced faith. Prayer and fasting are good, but trusting in prayer or fasting as a source for victory is misplaced faith. The idea of these verses is simple. Trusting in anything, even good things, and not the complete victory Christ had accomplished at Calvary is misplaced faith and leads not to victory but defeat.

Another important aspect is found in John 15. John speaks of the vine and how a branch cannot bear fruit unless it abides, dwells, remains attached to and depends on the vine. The Vine is Jesus Christ. The fruit is the Holy Spirit manifesting Himself through the believer (See Galatians 5:22-23). The believer must continue to receive all his nourishment and strength from the Vine, Jesus Christ. The believer cannot bear fruit or even survive spiritually without this relationship of dependency and trust with the Vine, Jesus Christ.

****

In the spring of 1998 during a week of revival services at our church, the Holy Spirit spoke to me in a clear and concise way. My wife and I were sitting in the balcony of the church during the preaching of the Word and the Holy Spirit said to me, "Learn what it means to be in Christ." That was it. That was the answer to my prayer for deliverance. But what did it mean? Wasn't I already "in Christ" when I was born again? "In Christ," What does it mean?

As I sit here writing, I realize it has been over 14 years since the Holy Spirit revealed this simple truth to me. To be "in Christ," I must be immersed into Jesus; I must dwell in Jesus; I must abide in Him; I must wholly depend upon Him in every area of my life.

This great amazing truth that the Holy Spirit revealed to me that evening in 1998 was not an easy truth to follow. First, I had to learn what it means to be in Christ. I thought I knew what it meant to be in Christ. I knew intellectually what it meant to be in Christ. After all, I learned all about water baptism when I was baptized at 13. Water baptism simply means I have dedicated my life, my entire life, to Jesus Christ as my Lord and Savior.

It symbolizes that just as Jesus Christ died, was buried, and rose again on the third day, I too am to die to my old self, be buried with Him, and will one day rise just as Jesus Christ rose from the dead. In reality, when we accept Jesus as our Savior and Lord, we become a new creation in Christ, the old is gone the new has come. (See 2 Corinthians 5:17). Water baptism symbolizes an outward manifestation of an inward commitment to serve Jesus Christ. It is a profession of faith to the world indicating your life will reflect honor and lift up Jesus in every way for the rest of your life.

I had many questions for God about what it meant to be "in Christ." So I went to the Book, the only Book of truth, the very Word of God. I searched the Scriptures, not intellectually but relationally. I read from cover to cover God's letter of love to me. I studied it. I asked God to reveal Himself to me and give me understanding of what it meant to be "in Christ."

The Bible is a very interesting book. Of course, it is the very Word of God. God is great, awesome, and powerful, and the words He speaks are full of wisdom, knowledge, and truth. Sometimes as meager human beings, we think we have attained great knowledge and skill and have great superiority in our thinking. Yet compared to God, we are like ants in our understanding. What impresses me about God is the simplicity of His Word, which helps me to know that God knows what is best. Many times we tend to confuse this wisdom with our great so-called understanding of big theological terms and religious activity. When God spoke to me saying, "Learn what it means to be in Christ," it was simple yet profound.

By Webster's definition the word *in* is defined as being "located inside or within–that is, in position, operations or power." To be "in Christ" would imply to be located inside Christ, in position, operations, and power. I was not living my life this way. I was not letting God's power flow through me in such a way as to bring glory and honor to Him. I was not giving the Holy Spirit control to operate His power in my life. I was trying to create my own fruit instead of letting the Holy Spirit bear fruit within me.

For example: I learned in Sunday school class when I was a child that "the fruit the Spirit is love, joy, peace, patience, kindness goodness, faithfulness, and self-control. Against such things there is no law" (Galatians 5:22-23). I was taught we must learn to love, be joyful, have peace, patience, etc. However I do not remember being taught that the Holy Spirit is the One who brings forth this fruit. It was all about what *I* must produce and not what God produces. This thinking was no different than that of a Pharisee during the time of Christ. I do not have to create this fruit; I do not have to try to love someone else. The Holy Spirit working in me produces the fruit of love in my life.

The Scripture tells us as believers in Christ to love one another. However, I am limited by my ability to really love. Only the Holy Spirit can produce the kind of genuine love God requires of us in loving one another. I must allow Him to love through me. I love others, not because they deserve it or because of my self-will, but because God's character of love flows through me and demonstrates love to that person, whether it be a friend or an enemy, a neighbor or a co-worker.

Love is more than the emotion, more than a physical contact. The love the world offers is very limited in its scope, but the love God produces in us is deeper than human expression of love. The Bible teaches in Corinthians 13 that love is kind, patient, keeps no records of wrong, it does not envy, and is not jealous to name a few of its characteristics. Godly love exhibits all of these characteristics all of the time. I cannot do these things in my own ability and knowledge. I need God to work within me to produce this fruit of love in my life. This unique love from God is called *agape* love, which is only produced by the Holy Spirit and the non-believer cannot create it. There are people in the world who can demonstrate all other kinds of love - sexual, family, and brotherly love - to some degree. Those are reflections of God's love. However, I cannot genuinely love as God loves his people, as God loves the world, without the Holy Spirit's manifestation of agape love through me. Agape love is not a fruit of my own effort or me, but a fruit of the Holy Spirit. Jesus said "A new commandment I give unto you, that ye love (agape) on another: as I have loved you, that ye also love one another. By this shall all men know that ye are my disciples, if ye have love (agape) one to another" (John 13:34-35). Therefore, my dependency upon the Holy Spirit is absolutely essential for the demonstration of this love.

Slowly I learned that to be "in Christ" is to be applied to more than just salvation and the Holy Spirit is more than just speaking in other tongues.

CHAPTER 15

Hope

Why art thou cast down, O my soul?
and why art thou disquieted in me?
hope thou in God.
Psalm 42:5

There is a beautiful story in the Bible of how God shows mercy to those who desire to do right. Rahab was a prostitute in the city of Jericho at the time when the Israelites were about to cross over the Jordan and conquer the land. Fear had fallen on all the people of Jericho and all hope was lost. Rahab upon the other hand had a plan to totally submit to God's will for her life. When the Israelite spies were sent to Jericho, she hid them, protected them, and told them of Jericho's fear. She also asked for a promise that when Israel attacked, she and her family would be spared in return for her assistance. The spies agreed to her request and told her to hang a scarlet cord used for their escape in the window. When God defeated Jericho, Rahab and her family were the only people spared and they integrated into the Israelite camp. The gospel of Matthew tells us that she married Salmon who became the father of Boaz, who became the father of Obed, who became the father of Jesse, who became the father of David, the king of Israel. It was through this lineage that the Messiah would come. (See Matthew 1:5-6, 17).

What is so amazing about this story is the faith Rahab placed in the God of Israel. Not only did she realize she was about to lose everything in Jericho, but also that her only hope was obedience to Israel's God. The scarlet cord represents the blood sacrifice of Christ, which redeems us all from death and destruction if we accept it by faith. Rahab protected the spies and God repaid her with honor to be a part of Israel and ultimately part of the lineage of the Messiah, Israel's greatest hope. Her faith in Israel's God gave her hope and life. The cross of Christ Jesus gives hope to those who trust in Him.

****

When God spoke to me, He gave me a desperately needed hope. My desire to serve Him and to do His will increased my desire to obey Him and love Him, which manifested itself through my desire to return to involvement in ministry. I began seeking the Lord for guidance and direction. I knew the calling of God was on my life and I would not be happy or content unless I was fulfilling His will. After praying about it for several months, the Lord spoke to my heart and told me to attend a particular smaller church. I did not know the pastor or anyone attending this church.

The first Sunday my beautiful wife and I attended this church, the service and sermon were good. I arranged to meet with the pastor before the Sunday evening service. I shared with the pastor that I felt God had told me to come and get involved with this church specifically. As a wise pastor, he listened and told me that he would be glad to give it some time, pray about it, and as the Lord led, he would give me opportunity. For the next couple of months, I participated in worship in the regular church services. Then one day the pastor asked me if I would open the morning service and evening service with announcements, prayer, and Scripture reading. I gladly jumped at the opportunity and humbly did my very best to be sensitive to the Holy Spirit and conform to the pastor's set pattern. It was a joy to be involved in ministry, to pray with people, and to be useful to God again. Then one day while sitting on the platform before the service began, the pastor asked if I would like to be the youth pastor. This was surprising because I wasn't aware of any youth in the church at the time. So basically, I would be starting with no youth. I told the pastor I would pray about it, think about it, and talk with my wife about the opportunity and get back with him.

We decided to follow the Lord's leading to accept the challenge of youth pastors with no youth to preach to or to shepherd. We decided to have the youth services on Saturday nights and advertised. On the Wednesday evening before our kick - off service, I talked with a teenager wandering around the church parking lot. I invited him to be part of the youth service we were to have that weekend. He said he had heard about it, but was planning for some of his friends to come over for some pizza and fun and spend the night at his house to celebrate his birthday. I offered to buy the pizza if he would come out Saturday night and bring all of his friends to help me kick off youth service. Food is always a good motivator for teenagers. He came and brought nine of his friends to the very first service.

I was green concerning youth ministry and had many misunderstandings or misconceptions of what a youth pastor should be like. After all, I had certain expectations of how church people should act, and these were not church people. Actually, most of them had never even gone to church. Some of them cursed and had very blatant attitudes. However, I was very adamant in my conviction of Jesus Christ, and preaching His love and salvation to all mankind. So in some respects, we were perfectly matched.

The Lord blessed my efforts with the youth ministry for the next 15 months. Our youth ministry averaged about 13 and at times as many as 25 or 30 came out. Several teenagers accepted Jesus Christ as Savior and were baptized in water for which I give God all the glory.

Although I was actively involved in ministry and reapplying for my ministerial credentials, I continued learning what it meant to be "in Christ." Being preoccupied in ministry, working fulltime, and trying to build a strong marriage was very time consuming. At times my wife and I put our TV in the closet in order to have quiet time to spending time alone with God in prayer and reading or building our relationship with one another. It was a good time for me as I continued to learn how to live victoriously.

CHAPTER 16

Death of Self

And he said to them all, If any man will come after me,
let him deny himself, and
take up his cross daily, and follow me.
Luke 9:23

Death is required of the believer. To *die to self* means to no longer have a personal influence. Everyone who is a follower of Christ Jesus must die to himself or herself, and let Jesus, who is life, resurrect them. This is a difficult process because we are used to doing things our way, living out our personal dreams, fulfilling our own individual wishes. I had to learn total dependency on God.

To deny self means to disown and to abstain from my own way of life in order to gain eternal life. Jesus said, "To know the only true God and His son, who He has sent, is life eternal" (John 17:3). God had to become greater than me in my life.

Although all people have the opportunity to follow Jesus Christ as their Savior and Lord, not everyone does this. The gospel is free to all, yet not everyone is willing to make the sacrifice of self. The key sin of man is exaltation of self. Self-will, self-determination, self-effort all ring with the emphasis of me, me, me. When Jesus tells us to deny self, it speaks of our own ability to save ourselves, deliver ourselves, and sanctify ourselves.

Next Jesus points us to the cross, which is the only means of presenting us holy and acceptable to God. It was at the cross Jesus "Who of God is made unto us wisdom, and righteousness, and sanctification, and redemption" (1 Corinthians 1:30). Everything we need is found at the cross! This is so "that no flesh should glory in his presence" (1 Corinthians 1:29). The cross is the object of our faith.

It is important to realize that this is a daily trust. You can't just believe God once then do your own thing. Your daily focus must be on the finished work done at Calvary.

It is only after we deny our own abilities and focus on the finished work of Christ at Calvary on a daily basis that we can actually follow Him and be obedient. This is the only path to victory. Any other method of victory will be short-lived and will not be successful.

****

After about a year of youth ministry, the Lord began speaking to me about pursuing a lead pastor position in a small church. I had really begun to love these teenagers as if they were my very own "flock," but the Lord had brought in other leaders. One leader, especially sensitive to the moving of the Holy Spirit, took the position and led the youth to the next level of spirituality when I left.

I had always desired to pastor a church. When I

preach, I can sense the presence of God in me and I know I have an anointing to preach and teach His Word. I started to send resume's to various churches, which were looking for full-time pastors. I received a few responses. A church in northern Missouri invited my wife and me for a weekend to preach Sunday services with an election to be held after the evening service. I did not get the position. I was severely disappointed for three reasons: (1) I saw no other possibilities open; (2) I had resigned my position as youth pastor, and I did not know where to go next; and (3) it was my birthday, and this was not a good birthday present. So I went back to delivering pizza.

CHAPTER 17

Grace

And he said unto me, My grace is sufficient for thee:
for my strength is made perfect in weakness.
Most gladly therefore will I rather glory in my infirmities,
that the power of Christ may rest upon me.
2 Corinthians 12:9

Paul was a man with many talents and gifts. He was a man who was given great revelations, visions of heaven, and achievements few could match. He was called to be an apostle of Jesus Christ. He had great zeal, an illustrious education, and many reasons to place confidence in self. Yet he learned the value of considering all these things as dung.

God reminded Paul that it was only through his weaknesses that God could be glorified. This is not an inability to do things, but a matter of dependency on who is doing it. It is the God's intention to make us weaker, that is, less self-reliant, and more dependent upon Christ for everything. John the Baptist said, "He must increase, but I must decrease" (John 3:30). God's greatest act of grace-goodness to undeserving man; unmerited favor– was done at Calvary's cross. It was enough to give us the victorious life.

Only God's grace gives us the ability to do anything at all. We must depend upon this grace for everything. Without this total dependency upon God for everything and faith focused on Christ's finished work, we will never gain the power for victory and never experience the life God has for us.

****

It is encouraging to know that the Lord orders the steps of a righteous man. (See Psalms 37:23, 85:13). The day after returning from the failed trip to northern Missouri, I returned to work my job at the pizza restaurant. I met a friend who was the pastor of a small church in Cave Springs, Missouri. He informed me he was leaving the church and it would be available for a new pastor. I knew right then this is where God wanted me. I had no doubt in my mind, my heart, and my spirit that this was God's direction.

A few days later, I spoke with my pastor and told him of my interest in the pastoral position in Cave Springs. He told me to pray and seek the Lord's guidance. About 10 days later, I confirmed with him that my wife and I believed this was where God wanted us. He set up a time for me to preach Sunday services with the understanding that in the Sunday evening service he would install me as pastor.

Cave Springs Assembly of God had a congregation of only seven adult members, but it had a dynamic youth ministry. The volunteer youth pastor was a student from a local Bible college, who had a fire and zeal to reach young people for the Lord. At times, about

30 teenagers met on Wednesday nights–many more in number than the adults. The founding pastor lived nearby and he reminisced with me of how the church started, grew, and shrank over the years. He too wanted to see it revitalized. I was ready. I was determined. I was motivated. I was challenged.

As the pastor of this church, I endeavored to preach, teach, and depend totally upon the Holy Spirit, being sensitive to His leading. The Lord had showed me the way of deliverance for my addiction. As I preached week after week, service after service, the biblical foundation for this deliverance became more apparent my life. I preached the deliverance of the Lord; I preached salvation; and I preach yielding to the Holy Spirit. In the 27 months I was pastor at Cave Springs, I had the privilege of leading nine people to the Lord and baptizing six new converts in water. To God is all the glory due.

When I was preaching, and when I was shepherding the flock, I felt the anointing and presence of God. I was in my element. I was in the right place at the right time, serving God with all my heart. I was a full-time employee, a full-time unpaid pastor, and a full-time husband. By the end of my time there, I felt like I had matured in my relationship with Jesus Christ.

I had some challenging experiences while serving as a pastor in Cave Springs. There were times when I had to show tough love and had to make difficult decisions in relation to members and leaders. God, through His grace, helped me and was there to guide me through the difficult waters.

In late 2003, following the advice from my presbyter, I resigned in good standing. My wife and I started attending a church in Springfield. The pastor was aware of my situation concerning my former church and opened up his arms to my wife and me. However, genuine faith will always be tested.

Back in the mid-90s when I first confessed to my wife about my addiction to pornography, she had confided in a co-worker about the situation, seeking advice as to what to do. This co-worker knew the pastor of the church we were currently attending and felt obligated to tell the pastor of my former addiction. This concerned him, especially since I was a credentialed minister, attending his church, and interested in doing some teaching or preaching. The pastor called me into his office one day and asked me directly if I was still struggling with this addiction. I told him I was living victoriously with an occasional struggle because I was still learning to walk by faith. The addiction did not have dominion in my life and my triumphs were much greater than my losses. The Bible teaches dependency upon God, the Holy Spirit and faith placed properly in the redemptive and sanctifying work of Christ on the cross. I am reminded of the Scriptures in Psalms 37:23-24, which says "The steps of a good man are ordered by the LORD: and he delighteth in his way. Though he fall, he shall not be utterly cast down: for the LORD upholdeth him with his hand."

In the years since, dying to self, depending on the Holy Spirit, and actually believing the Word of God has dramatically increased my faith. The foundation of my victory is centered upon the cross of Jesus Christ. When Jesus died for my sins, He also produced my victory, therefore providing a way for me to live an overcoming life. Jesus conquered the power of sin once and for all! It's not because of what I do, but because of what He has done that I am free. I have to believe with all my heart that when Jesus died for my victory, the victory was total. I do not add to or take away from the sacrifice Jesus made for me. To be "in Christ" means the likeness of Jesus is so incorporated in me that when people see me, they see Christ and not me. To be "in Christ" means total, absolute dependency upon the Holy Spirit. It requires me to abide within Him every day, every hour, every minute.

I am still learning how to walk by faith and not by sight. I am still fighting the good fight of faith and learning how to depend on God for other areas in my life but sin no longer has dominion over me.

In my life, I have experienced rebellion, self-righteousness, arrogance, pride, and self-dependency. But now, by the grace of God I have begun to learn how to die and deny self. I have learned what it means to live victorious over sin and not allow its dominion in my life. I have learned the necessity of total dependence upon the Holy Spirit and, in a small way, how He works. I have learned to totally believe in the finished work of Christ and its total sufficiency. I have begun to know what it means to be "in Christ."

EPILOGUE

I sat alone in the darkness trapped by my own mistakes and decisions–surrounded by rocks and cold. I wondered what else I could have done to defeat this relentless enemy. I could still hear their evil voices searching, desiring my destruction. I had nothing left with which to fight. I was tired, weary, and saddened by the fact that there seemed to be no more hope to cling to. I felt abandoned by my commander.

Then there was an explosion, which threw me to the other side of the cavern. Smoke and dust from the rubble filled my lungs as I tried to regain my position. The enemy had found me and all I could do was give them all the bullets I had left in my weapon. But it was not enough, there were too many of them. I was shot in the leg, then the arm. I stumbled and fell to my knees. The enemy grabbed me and bound me with chains. I struggled to get away with no success. I was too weak and they were too strong. They placed the chains around my neck, arms, and legs. I was bound like a slave. My movement was limited; the bullets in my limbs intensified the pain. I was defeated. They mocked me as they began to drag me away. I prayed to God for mercy for I knew I would receive no mercy from the enemy.

Then suddenly, the ground began to shake. The rocks split apart and I saw light piercing though the cracks. I heard the screams of the enemy crying in deathly fear as rocks crushed their bodies, silencing their lives, and forcing some of them to retreat. All around me, I saw my enemy look at one another in horrifying fear and dismay while falling to their knees. As my enemy tried to stand, they kept falling again to their knees. The power of the light blinded my enemy. Then I saw my commander–strong and victorious–standing in front of me. The chains that once bound me fell off and my strength returned to me. He reached out to my wounds and healed them. "Come and follow me," He said. I followed Him out of the depths of despair and depression. I followed Him out of the bondage of sin and addiction. Jesus, my Commander, had once and for all set me free.

When I was young, I built tunnels in the straw to defend myself from a secret enemy. Now, I need not defend myself for Jesus Christ is my strong tower, my fortress, and my defender against the enemy. Jesus Christ has defeated the enemy once and for all. The enemy has no dominion in my life, so now I can enjoy the thrill of victory instead of the agony of defeat.

AFTERWORD

The six requirements to live victoriously over any addiction or struggle are as follows

1. **<u>You must be born again.</u>**

Jesus put it plainly to Nicodemus one night when the two were conversing: *"Except a man be born again he cannot see the kingdom of God"* (John 3:3). Jesus then said, *"Except a man be born of water and of the Spirit, he cannot enter into the kingdom of God"* (John 3:5). This confused Nicodemus so he asked, *"How can these things be?"* (John 3:9) Then Jesus pointed to the example of Moses and how he *"lifted up the serpent in the wilderness, even so must the Son of man be lifted up: That whosoever believeth in Him should not perish but have eternal life"* (John 3:14-15).

To be *born again* means that one has experienced a dramatic, life-changing event. Man is in rebellion against God because of his sin. The Bible says: *"For all have sinned, and come short of the glory of God"* (Romans 3:23). The legal penalty of sin is death. (See Romans 6:23). In order to have communion with God again, the penalty had to be paid. Jesus, who is God, Incarnate, came through the Virgin Mary and became a man. Due to the fact that He was conceived of the Holy Spirit and not of natural man

He was perfect in every way, sinless and was qualified to pay the penalty of our sin. He suffered a brutal crucifixion *"To give his life a ransom for many"* (Matthew 20:28). Jesus could not die because he was perfect *"…and in Him is no sin"* (1 John 3:5). But Jesus said, *"Therefore doth my Father love me, because I lay down my life, that I might take it again"* (John 10:17). You might ask why God would do such a thing for me. Jesus puts it this way: "*For God so loved the world that he gave his only begotten Son, that whosoever believeth in Him should not perish, but have everlasting life. For God sent not his Son into the world to condemn the world; but that the world through Him might be saved* (John 3:16-17). God's purpose was not to condemn mankind to eternal damnation, but to give life that *"…he might reconcile both unto God in one body by the cross, having slain the enmity thereby"* (Eph 2:16).

So we see from the Bible that we have all sinned against God. Jesus paid the penalty for that sin by laying down His life for us on the Cross so we could be reconciled to God. He did this because He loves us so very much.

This explains the condition of man, but not how to be born again. To be born again or "saved" from sin, we must go again to the Bible. Romans 10:9-10 says: *"That if thou shalt confess with thy mouth the Lord Jesus, and shalt believe in thine heart that God hath raised Him from the dead, thou shalt be saved. For with the heart man believeth unto righteousness; and with the mouth confession is made unto salvation."* To put it in simple terms, you must believe Jesus died on the Cross for your sins, and He will forgive your sins if you ask, and you must confess or commit to following Jesus the rest of your life. This is how you can be "saved" or born again.

One of the results of salvation is a new creation. "*Therefore if any man be in Christ, he is a new creature: [creation] old things are passed away; behold all things are become new*" (2 Corinthians 5:17). God does not rehabilitate; He gets rid of the old and creates new.

When a man builds a house, he must begin with a solid foundation. If the foundation is faulty, the house that is built on it, no matter how beautiful and majestic, will not survive the onslaught of natural forces. So it is with our contaminated flesh. Sinful man cannot stand up to the holiness of God. When we yield ourselves to God, He transforms us and creates a house built on a sure foundation, the perfection of His Son Jesus Christ. God can then dwell and therefore work in us "*…to be conformed to the image of his Son*" (Rom 8:29), i.e. one acceptable to God.

Multiple millions of people over the centuries have experienced this new birth. Drug addicts, prostitutes, murderers, homosexuals, gamblers, thieves, liars and selfish people, to name just a few, have experience the power of Jesus Christ forgiving their sins and giving them new, abundant life. Broken homes have been put back together. Where there was hopelessness and despair, there is now peace, love, and hope. This salvation or new birth is available to all, but each individual must receive this gift from God personally by faith.

You might ask why this is important for total deliverance from addiction. The answer is simple. First, addiction is a result of sin. You cannot fully overcome addiction in your own strength–no matter how hard you try–without the blood of Christ cleansing you of your sin. (This is why 12 step programs are unsuccessful). Secondly, you need the working of the Holy Spirit (God) working in you to overcome. God the Holy Spirit cannot dwell in you unless your sin is totally gone. This is done by faith in Jesus Christ.

2. **<u>You must believe God's Word.</u>**

You are what you believe.

Abraham is considered the great patriarch of the Jewish race. He not only obeyed God and moved to the land of Canaan, but he did great things for God as a result of his obedience. He fathered a nation and taught them about the one true God. But what really made him great is that he believed God! The Bible says "He believed in the LORD; and he (God) counted it to him for righteousness. (Genesis 15:6; Romans 4:3).

The Holy Bible is the very Word of God. *"All scripture is given by inspiration of God, and is profitable for doctrine, for reproof, for correction, for instruction in righteousness: That the man of God may be perfect, throughly furnished unto all good works"* (2 Timothy 3:16-17). There is no error when God speaks. God is all-knowing, all-powerful and ever-present. When He speaks he does not and cannot lie. The Word of God is absolute truth.

Matthew 18:3-4 says, *"Verily I say unto you, 'Except ye be converted, and become as little children, ye shall not enter into the kingdom of heaven. Whosoever therefore shall humble himself as this little child, the same is greatest in the kingdom of heaven."* The secret to believing the Word of God is to come as a little child. A one year old child does not doubt, but just believes. A child believes his father has his best interests in mind. A child totally trusts his father. Jesus wants us to have the mindset of a child and totally believe Him.

God has given to us His Word so we can have a tool to guide our faith in Him. The Bible is to be read, studied, memorized, and hidden in our hearts. But even more important is that we must believe the Bible. When we believe His written Word, it will give us life, hope, and peace.

You must believe the Word of God. *"Thy word have I hid in mine heart, that I might not sin against thee"* (Psalms 119:11). The Word of God purifies, cleanses, renews the mind, transforms the soul and centers our attention on the cross. The Bible is the redemption story of man and it reminds us of our fragilities and God's great mercy and love. It gives us hope, peace, joy and comfort.

3. **<u>You must have what Jesus accomplished on the cross (His finished work) as the object of your faith.</u>**

It is easy for people to trust in other things rather than God. People trust in religion, organizations, government, family, and even themselves for a variety of reasons. These things have their place and benefits. However when it comes to addictions, there is only one object of trust you must have and that is the *finished work of Christ* done on the cross. Paul the apostle placed this emphasis on the cross: *"For Christ sent me not to baptize, but to preach the gospel: not with wisdom of words, lest the cross of Christ should be made of none effect. For the preaching of the cross is to them that perish foolishness; but unto us which are saved it is the power of God"* (1 Corinthians 1:17-18). Also in chapter two of First Corinthians: *"For I determined not to know any thing among you, save Jesus Christ, and Him crucified. And I was with you in weakness, and in fear, and in much trembling. And my speech and my preaching was not with enticing words of man's wisdom, but in demonstration of the Spirit and of power: That your faith should not stand in the wisdom of men, but in the power of God"* (1 Corinthians 2:2-5). Paul, one of the greatest missionaries of the early church, wanted to make it very clear that his message was singular in nature: Jesus and Him crucified or the message of the cross!

Paul believed in the *finished work* of Christ so strongly that he boldly acknowledged he was *"not ashamed of the gospel of Christ: for it is the power of God unto salvation to everyone that believeth"* (Romans 1:16). He understood it to be the power of God unto salvation to those who believe. The word salvation can also be translated "delivered." The idea is that God delivered us from sin and the bondage of sin. So Paul is saying that what Jesus accomplished on the cross is where the power of God can be found for your deliverance from *any* addiction because addiction is a result of sin!

Now that we know the value of the *finished work of Christ,* let us look at how we can apply it to our lives. *"Know ye not, that so many of us as were baptized into Jesus Christ were baptized into his death? Therefore we are buried with Him by baptism into death: that like as Christ was raised up from the dead by the glory of the Father, even so we also should walk in newness of life. For if we have been planted together in the likeness of his death, we shall be also in the likeness of his resurrection"* (Romans 6:3-5). It is obvious that this passage of Scripture can and does speak of Salvation. For when we believe in what Jesus did for us by dying for us we are saved.

However, in the context of the sixth chapter of Romans, it also speaks of sanctification, which deals with addiction. *"Knowing this, that our old man is crucified with Him, that the body of sin might be destroyed, that henceforth we should not serve sin. For he that is dead is freed from sin"* (Romans 6:6-7). And *"For sin shall not have dominion over you: for ye are not under the law, but under grace"* (Romans 6:14). "Should not serve sin" and "sin shall not have dominion over you" speaks of the progressive work of God in the believer or sanctification. In other words, the everyday struggles we go through in living for God. So we see in these verses the emphasis on what Jesus did on the cross and our belief in that *finished work.*

When a person is addicted to something, and it could be anything, it is a result of sin. The reason it is sin is because of trust in self or "I" can overcome this. The Bible says, *"…for whatsoever is not of faith is sin"* (Romans 14:23). Faith has to do with trust and dependency in God, therefore when we do not trust God we default to trusting in self and that is sin. It could be the sin of unbelief, the sin of rebellion, or the sin of pride. God expects us to walk by faith, and not by our own senses, earthly wisdom, or personal experience.

As a new creature in Christ, we must believe all that happened at Calvary. First Corinthians 1:30 tells us what happened at Calvary: *"But of Him are ye in Christ Jesus, who of God is made unto us wisdom, and righteousness, and sanctification, and redemption."* *Wisdom* in this verse speaks of our understanding of God's great gift. *Righteousness* speaks of God making us "not guilty", justified by Christ's blood to stand before Him, or as one person put it, "just-as-if-I-never-sinned." *Sanctification* speaks of the continual process of becoming holy like Christ through the working of the Holy Spirit in our lives. And finally, *redemption* speaks of being delivered, ransom paid, from our slavery to sin. Of course, all of this is accomplished through what Jesus did on the cross being the object or focus of our belief.

4. **<u>You must deny your own ability to overcome the addiction.</u>**

There is a wonderful example of denial of self in the Garden of Gethsemane when Jesus was about to be tortured, beaten, and crucified for the sins of mankind. He said, *"Father, if thou be willing, remove this cup from me: nevertheless not my will, but thine, be done"* (Luke 22:42). *"Not my will, but thine, be done"* speaks volumes of the attitude Christ had when going where He did not want to go. It is a willingness to do that which must be done at great personal sacrifice in order to achieve the purpose intended. The believer must realize that in order to overcome addiction, he must stop trying to do it himself.

Personally, it was wasn't until I realized I was in the way and had to stop trying myself to overcome that God was able to do His work. God will not share His glory with anyone!

Jesus put it this way: *"If any man will come after me, let him deny himself, and take up his cross daily, and follow me. For whosoever will save his life shall lose it: but whosoever will lose his life for my sake, the same shall save it"* (Luke 9:23-24). In other words, if you want to follow Jesus and receive all of His benefits, you must deny your own ability to earn or deserve them and trust in the *finished work* of Christ every day before you can follow Him. If you try to gain or save your life (overcome your addictions on your own) you will fail, but if you give it all over to God and do it His way, you will gain life.

This was a very difficult lesson for me personally. We all learn to depend on self as we grow up. We get a job to save up for a car, move out on our own, go to college. We pursue careers we think we will like, spouse we think we could live with, and a life that meets our dreams. We are trained from childhood to do this and this is not a bad thing. However, when it comes to addictions and overcoming sin, we must rely on a power greater than ourselves, Jesus Christ and He does not share His glory with anyone. "*That no flesh should glory in his presence*" (1 Corinthians 1:29) makes this point very clear. In other words, I had to stop trying to overcome and just believe that Jesus already overcame it on the cross for me and, therefore, trust Him for my deliverance.

So what does it mean to deny our own abilities? Consider these questions: Who do you really trust: yourself or God? Who are you really depending upon: yourself or God? Who do you really believe: yourself or God?

5. **<u>You must not add anything to the finished work of Christ</u>**

Overcoming sin with God's help will never work! Many people try to earn their deliverance or do things to overcome on their own. They even try to "help" God out by their effort or religious activities. This will always end in failure.

Early in my struggle, I tried to overcome my sin by avoiding certain places, holding myself accountable to another person, and removing all temptation from my presence. Among other things, I got more involved in church, read my Bible more, prayed more earnestly, and kept busy with other things. My determination and will to overcome was strong, yet these things only had a minimal effect and gave me only temporary relief. I still struggled and fell from grace.

Now there is nothing wrong with doing these things. Common sense would dictate that if you're an alcoholic, you shouldn't be visiting bars. But the issue is trust. Do you trust in these things? Are you trying to "earn" your deliverance by doing these things? This is the issue with many Christians. At best this can only lead to self-righteousness and hypocrisy. In other words, "Look what I have done to overcome," and man gets the credit.

When a person becomes "born again" or "saved," he comes to the conclusion that what Jesus did at the cross can save him from his sin. Only what Jesus did at the cross can deliver him from Hell, forgive him and give him eternal life. He places his faith exclusively in what Jesus did when he died for us. He acknowledges that Jesus died as a sacrifice for his sins and if he asks Him to take over Jesus will forgive him and give him a new life. He knows he cannot do anything to add to this, he must just trust in Jesus and believe His Word. It is not different when it comes to overcoming sin.

In Romans 7, Paul speaks of the purpose of the Law. It is to reveal to us how sinful we are. The Ten Commandments clearly show us our inability to live perfect before God. But as Christians we no longer live under the rules of the law. *"We are not under the law but grace"* (Romans 6:14). We live under the conviction of the Holy Spirit and thus are able to "*...fulfill the law of Christ*" (Galatians 6:2). Therefore, we no longer live as unto the law of "thou shall not do that" and "thou shall do this," but under grace.

By placing our trust in "things" to help God out, we are placing ourselves under law and adding to the *finished work* of Christ.

We cannot add anything to God's deliverance process. God requires absolute surrender and trust in Him. What Jesus did at the cross is sufficient. We must believe that the *finished work* is sufficient. Our dependency must be placed only in His accomplished *finished work*. This is the singular thing we must do. Trust, believe, have faith in Christ's *finished work*.

6. **You must yield to the Holy Spirit in everything.**

The Bible clearly teaches that we must *"Walk in the Spirit, and ye shall not fulfill the lust of the flesh"* (Galatians 5:16). What does that mean?

First, let's define what the "flesh" is. The flesh, or sinful nature, is that part of man that tends to want to do; is bent toward doing; evil. The Bible says the works of the flesh are *"Adultery, fornication* (harlotry and incest), *uncleanness* (impurity, sexual or moral), *lasciviousness* (looseness, promiscuous), *Idolatry, witchcraft, hatred* (hostility), *variance* (quarreling), *emulations* (jealousy and indignation), *wrath, strife, seditions* (divisive), *heresies, envyings, murders* (can include murder of character), *drunkenness, revellings* (partying or riots), *and such like"* (Galatians 5:19-21).

When a person becomes a genuine Christian, God makes the sinful nature become dormant. Paul puts it this way: *"Know ye not, that so many of us as were baptized into Jesus Christ were baptized into his death? Therefore we are buried with Him by baptism into death: that like as Christ was raised up from the dead by the glory of the Father, even so we also should walk in newness of life. For if we have been planted together in the likeness of his death, we shall be also in the likeness of his resurrection: Knowing this, that our old man is crucified with Him, that the body of sin might be destroyed, that henceforth we should not serve sin. For he that is dead is freed from sin…For sin shall not have dominion over you: for ye are not under the law, but under grace"* (Romans 6:3-7, 14). The flesh is only resurrected by law. Again Paul explains it: *"But sin, taking occasion by the commandment, [Law] wrought in me all manner of concupiscence. For without the law sin was dead. For I was alive without the law once: but when the commandment came, sin revived, and I died. And the commandment, which was ordained to life, I found to be unto death. For sin, taking occasion by the commandment, deceived me, and by it slew me*" (Romans 7:8-11). We also know from Scripture that *"The flesh lusteth against the Spirit, and the Spirit against the flesh: and these are contrary the one to the other: so that ye cannot do the things that ye would"* (Galatians 5:17). There is a battle for the Christian between living in the Spirit and the Flesh. The trick is keeping the flesh dormant. That can only be done by walking in the Spirit. To walk in the Spirit means to live like God does in thought and action. (However, it doesn't mean you are a god!)

If you feel condemnation or guilt, it is a sign that you are not walking in the Spirit. The Holy Spirit convicts, the devil condemns. The Bible says, *"There is therefore now no condemnation to them which are* ***in Christ Jesus****, who walk not after the flesh, but after the Spirit. For the law of the* ***Spirit of life*** *in Christ Jesus hath made me free from the law of sin and death"* (Romans 8:1-2). Notice the phrase "in Christ Jesus" and the "Spirit of life". The law of the Spirit of life is the only power greater than the law of sin and death. These are the two most powerful laws in the universe. The only way to permit the law of the Spirit of life to work in you is to be in Christ Jesus. The primary purpose of the Holy Spirit is to give life to the individual within the parameters of Christ's work. Life has to do with victory; sin has to do with death. This is God's prescribed order of victory.

To walk in the Spirit means to dwell with or be around, the Holy Spirit. It is the same concept as abiding in the vine which Jesus speaks of in John 15. We must dwell with the Spirit and be led or guided by Him. We must listen to Him, do what He says, and be totally obedient to Him. The Holy Spirit is a part of the Triune Godhead and equal with Jesus and the Father. They are in unison; One God in three persons. God does not do anything outside of the parameters of the *finished work* of Christ. He does not do anything contrary to the Word of God. We are to be in perfect union with Him.

When we do this, the flesh stays dormant and we walk in continuous victory. Addictions no longer control us. The flesh is dead and we are being *"Conformed to the image of his Son"* (Romans 8:29).

To recap, the six requirements to overcoming any addiction or struggle are as follows:

1. **You must be born again.**
2. **You must believe God's Word.**
3. **You must have what Jesus accomplished on the cross (His finished work) as the object of your faith.**
4. **You must deny your own ability to overcome the addiction.**
5. **You must not add anything to the finished work of Christ.**
6. **You must yield to the Holy Spirit in everything.**

Each requirement is necessary in order to overcome your addiction. You cannot pick and choose the requirements you want to do and ignore the rest. It is all or nothing, black or white, deliverance or bondage.

God desires that you be free from sin and the bondage of sin. If you follow all of these requirements you will live the victorious, overcoming life Jesus had promise when he said: *"If the Son therefore shall make you free, ye shall be free indeed"* (John 8:36).

www.ingramcontent.com/pod-product-compliance
Ingram Content Group UK Ltd.
Pitfield, Milton Keynes, MK11 3LW, UK
UKHW020241250726
13967UKWH00001B/490